DATE		

THE USE OF POETRY
AND THE USE OF CRITICISM

STUDIES IN
THE RELATION OF CRITICISM
TO POETRY IN ENGLAND

T. S. ELIOT

HARVARD UNIVERSITY PRESS
CAMBRIDGE, MASSACHUSETTS

The Preface to the Edition of 1964 is included
by arrangement with Faber and Faber Ltd.

Library of Congress Cataloging-in-Publication Data

Eliot, T. S. (Thomas Stearns), 1888–1965.
The use of poetry and the use of criticism.

(The Charles Eliot Norton lectures for 1932–33)
1. English poetry—History and criticism.
2. Criticism—Great Britain. I. Title. II. Series:
Charles Eliot Norton lectures; 1932–1933.
PR503.E45   1986   821'.009   86-11926
ISBN 0–674–93150–5

PREFACE TO THE
EDITION OF 1964

IT is said that Yeats had more than enough of
The Lake Isle of Innisfree as his anthology
piece. In my youth *La Figlia Che Piange* was favoured as the most innocuous of my poems, but
in later years I have been more fairly represented (though I should be glad to hear no more
of a bang and a whimper). But with my essays I
have not been so fortunate. Just as any student
of contemporary literature, putting pen to paper
about my criticism, is certain to pass an examination on it if he alludes to the 'dissociation of
sensibility' and the 'objective correlative', so every anthologist wishing to include a sample of my
essays will choose *Tradition and the Individual
Talent*—perhaps the most juvenile and certainly
the first to appear in print.

I reprint *The Use of Poetry and the Use of
Criticism* in the faint hope that one of these lectures may be taken instead of *Tradition and
the Individual Talent* by some anthologist of the
future. That, the best known of my essays,
appeared in 1917, when I had taken over
the assistant-editorship of *The Egoist* on Richard
Aldington's being called up for military service,
and before I had been asked to contribute to any
other periodical. The lectures which compose
the present book were written during the winter
of 1932–33. I had been honoured with appoint-
ment to the Charles Eliot Norton Professorship

PREFACE TO THE EDITION OF 1964

at Harvard—a position offered annually to some man of letters, American or European, for the period of one year. I did not find leisure to prepare the lectures until I arrived in Cambridge, Massachusetts, in the autumn of 1932, and so they had to be composed, under considerable pressure, during the period of my residence there. Nevertheless, after re-reading them twice, I found to my surprise that I was still prepared to accept them as a statement of my critical position.

My earliest critical essays, dating from a period when I was somewhat under the influence of Ezra Pound's enthusiasm for Remy de Gourmont, came to seem to me the product of immaturity—though I do not repudiate 'Tradition and the Individual Talent.' The eight lectures in this volume, in spite of the fact that some of them were written in the course of delivering the series, seem to me still valid. At least, I am ashamed neither of the style nor of the matter. Not having looked at them for many years, I found them, after two readings, acceptable enough for me to hope that republication in the present form may justify itself.

As for the opening paragraph of the first lecture, I should explain that the United States were at that moment on the eve of the presidential election which brought Franklin D. Roosevelt his first term of office.

T.S.E.

1963

CONTENTS

THE USE OF POETRY
AND THE USE OF CRITICISM

INTRODUCTION

"THE whole country is now excited by the political campaign, and in a condition of irrational emotion. The best of the prospect is that a reorganisation of parties seems not unlikely as an indirect result of the present contest between the Republicans and the Democrats. . . . But any radical change is not to be hoped for."

These words occur in a letter written by Charles Eliot Norton on September 24th, 1876. The present lectures will have no concern with politics; I have begun with a political quotation only as a reminder of the varied interests of the scholar and humanist whom this foundation commemorates. The lecturer on such a foundation is fortunate who can feel, as I do, sympathy and admiration for the man whose memory the lectures are intended to keep living. Charles Eliot Norton had the moral and spiritual qualities, of a stoic kind, which are possible without the benefits of revealed religion; and the mental gifts which are possible without genius. To do the useful thing, to say the courageous thing, to contemplate the beautiful thing: that is enough for one man's life. Few men have known better than he how to give just place to the claims of the public and of the private life; few men have had better opportunity, few of those having the opportunity have availed themselves of it better than he. The usual politician, the man of public affairs, is rarely able to go to the "public place" without assuming the "public face": Norton always preserved his privacy. And living as he did in a non-Christian society, and in a world which, as he saw it on both sides of the Atlantic, showed signs of decay, he maintained the standards of the humanity and humanism that he knew. He was able, even at an early age, to look upon the passing order without regret, and towards the coming order without hope. In a letter of December 1869 he speaks more strongly and more comprehensively than in that which I have quoted:

The future is very dark in Europe, and to me it looks as if we were entering upon a period quite new in history, — one in which the questions on which parties will divide, and from which outbreak after outbreak of passion and violence will arise, will not longer be political but immediately social. . . . Whether our period of economic enterprise, unlimited competition, and unrestrained individualism, is the highest stage of human progress is to me very doubtful; and sometimes, when I see the existing conditions of European (to say nothing of American) social order, bad as they are for the mass alike of upper and lower classes, I wonder whether our civilisation can maintain itself against the forces which are banding together for the destruction of many of the institutions in which it is embodied, or whether we are not to have another period of decline, fall, and ruin and revival, like that of the first thirteen hundred years of our era. It would not grieve me much to know that this were to be the case. No man who knows what society at the present day really is, but must agree that it is not worth preserving on its present basis.[1]

[1] My quotations from Norton's letters are taken from the *Life and Letters of Charles Eliot Norton* (Houghton, Mifflin: 2 vols.).

These are words to which many who approach contemporary problems with more dogmatic assumptions than Norton's can give assent. Yet for him the
permanent importance of literature if not of dogma
was a fixed point. The people which ceases to care for
its literary inheritance becomes barbaric; the people
which ceases to produce literature ceases to move in
thought and sensibility. The poetry of a people takes
its life from the people's speech and in turn gives life
to it; and represents its highest point of consciousness, its greatest power and its most delicate sensibility.

In these lectures I have to deal as much or more
with criticism of poetry as with poetry itself; and my
subject is not merely the relation of criticism to poetry, if by that we assume that we know already
what poetry is, and does, and is for. Indeed, a good
part of criticism has consisted simply in the pursuit
of answers to these questions. Let me start with
the supposition that we do not know what poetry is,
or what it does or ought to do, or of what use it is; and
try to find out, in examining the relation of poetry
and criticism, what the use of both of them is. We
may even discover that we have no very clear idea of
what *use* is; at any rate we had better not assume
that we know.

I shall not begin with any general definition of what
is and what is not poetry, or any discussion of whether
poetry need be always in verse, or any consideration
of the difference between the poetry-verse antithesis
and the poetry-prose antithesis. Criticism, however,

may be separated from the beginning not into two kinds, but according to two tendencies. I assume that criticism is that department of thought which either seeks to find out what poetry is, what its use is, what desires it satisfies, why it is written and why read, or recited; or which, making some conscious or unconscious assumption that we do know these things, assesses actual poetry. We may find that good criticism has other designs than these; but these are the ones which it is allowed to profess. Criticism, of course, never does find out what poetry is, in the sense of arriving at an adequate definition; but I do not know of what use such a definition would be if it were found. Nor can criticism ever arrive at any final appraisal of poetry. But there are these two theoretical limits of criticism: at one of which we attempt to answer the question "what is poetry?" and at the other "is this a good poem?" No theoretic ingenuity will suffice to answer the second question, because no theory can amount to much which is not founded upon a direct experience of good poetry; but on the other hand our direct experience of poetry involves a good deal of generalising activity.

The two questions, which represent the most abstract formulation of what is far from being an abstract activity, imply each other. The critic who remains worth reading has asked, if he has only imperfectly answered, both questions. Aristotle, in what we possess of his writings upon poetry, does, I think, quicken our appreciation of the Greek tragic dramatists; Coleridge, in his defence of the poetry of Wordsworth, is led into generalisations about poetry which are of the greatest interest; and Wordsworth, in his explanation of his own poetry, makes assertions about the nature of poetry which, if excessive, have a wider bearing than even he may have realised. Mr. I. A. Richards, who ought to know, if anyone does, what equipment the scientific critic needs, tells us that "both a passionate knowledge of poetry and a capacity for dispassionate psychological analysis" are required. Mr. Richards, like every serious critic of poetry, is a serious moralist as well. His ethics, or theory of value, is one which I cannot accept; or rather, I cannot accept any such theory which is erected upon purely individual-psychological foundations. But his psychology of the poetic experience is based upon his own experience of poetry, as truly as his theory of value arises out of his psychology. You may be dissatisfied with his philosophical conclusions but still believe (as I do) in his discriminating taste in poetry. But if on the other hand you had no faith in the critic's ability to tell a good poem from a bad one, you would put little reliance upon the validity of his theories. In order to analyse the enjoyment and appreciation of a good poem, the critic must have experienced the enjoyment, and he must convince us of his taste. For the experience of enjoying a bad poem while thinking it is a good one is very different from that of enjoying a good poem.

We do expect the critic who theorises to know a good poem when he sees it. It is not always true that a person who knows a good poem when he sees it can

tell us why it is a good poem. The experience of poetry, like any other experience, is only partially trans-
latable into words; to begin with, as Mr. Richards
says, "it is never what a poem *says* that matters, but
what it *is*." And we know that some people who are
inarticulate, and cannot say why they like a poem,
may have deeper and more discriminating sensibility
than some others who can talk glibly about it; we
must remember too that poetry is not written simply
to provide material for conversation. Even the most
accomplished of critics can, in the end, only point to
the poetry which seems to him to be the real thing.
Nevertheless, our talking about poetry is a part of, an
extension of, our experience of it; and as a good deal
of thinking has gone to the making of poetry, so a
good deal may well go to the study of it. The rudi-
ment of criticism is the ability to select a good poem
and reject a bad poem; and its most severe test is of
its ability to select a good *new* poem, to respond properly to a new situation. The experience of poetry, as
it develops in the conscious and mature person, is not
merely the sum of the experiences of good poems. Education in poetry requires an organisation of these
experiences. There is not one of us who is born with,
or who suddenly acquires at puberty or later, an in-
fallible discrimination and taste. The person whose
experience is limited is always liable to be taken in by
the sham or the adulterate article; and we see generation after generation of untrained readers being taken
in by the sham and the adulterate in its own time —
indeed preferring them, for they are more easily as-

similable than the genuine article. Yet a very large number of people, I believe, have the native capacity for enjoying *some* good poetry: how much, or how many degrees of capacity may profitably be distinguished, is not part of my present purpose to enquire. It is only the exceptional reader, certainly, who in the course of time comes to classify and compare his experiences, to see one in the light of others; and who, as his poetic experiences multiply, will be able to understand each more accurately. The element of enjoyment is enlarged into appreciation, which brings a more intellectual addition to the original intensity of feeling. It is a second stage in our understanding of poetry when we no longer merely select and reject, but organise. We may even speak of a third stage, one of reorganisation; a stage at which a person already educated in poetry meets with something new in his own time, and finds a new pattern of poetry arranging itself in consequence.

This pattern, which we form in our own minds out of our own reading of poetry that we have enjoyed, is a kind of answer, which we make each for himself, to the question "what is poetry?" At the first stage we find out what poetry is by reading it and enjoying some of what we read; at a later stage our perception of the resemblances and differences between what we read for the first time and what we have already enjoyed itself contributes to our enjoyment. We learn what poetry is — if we ever learn — from reading it; but one might say that we should not be able to recognise poetry in particular unless we had an innate idea of poetry in general. At any rate, the question "what is poetry?" issues quite naturally from our experience of poems. Even, therefore, although we may admit that few forms of intellectual activity seem to have less to show for themselves, in the course of history, in the way of books worth reading, than does criticism, it would appear that criticism, like any philosophica-activity, is inevitable and requires no justificationl To ask "what is poetry?" is to posit the critical function.

I suppose that to many people the thought must have occurred, that at some periods when great poetry was written there was no written criticism; and that in some periods in which much criticism has been written the quality of the poetry has been inferior. This fact has suggested an antithesis between the critical and the creative, between critical ages and creative ages; and it is sometimes thought that criticism flourishes most at times when creative vigour is in defect. It is with such a prejudice in mind that people have coupled with "critical ages" the adjective "Alexandrian." Several gross assumptions underlie this prejudice, including a confusion between several different things, and between works of very different quality, included under "criticism." I am using the term "criticism" throughout these lectures, as I hope you will discover, with a pretty narrow extension. I have no desire to extenuate the vices of the vast number of books which pass by that designation, or to flatter the lazy habit of substituting, for a careful study of the texts, the assimilation of other people's opinions. If people only wrote when they had something to say, and never merely because they wanted to write a book, or because they occupied a position such that the writing of books was expected of them, the mass of criticism would not be wholly out of proportion to the small number of critical books worth reading. Nevertheless, those who speak as if criticism were an occupation of decadence, and a symptom, if not a cause, of the creative impotence of a people, isolate the circumstances of literature, to the extent of falsification, from the circumstances of life. Such changes as that from the epic poem composed to be recited to the epic poem composed to be read, or those which put an end to the popular ballad, are inseparable from social changes on a vast scale, such changes as have always taken place and always will. W. P. Ker, in his essay on "The Forms of English Poetry," observed that

The art of the Middle Ages generally is corporate and social; the sculpture, for example, as it is found on the great cathedrals. With the Renaissance the motive of poetry is changed. In the Middle Ages there is a natural likeness to the Greek conditions; after the Renaissance there is a conscious and intentional reproduction among the modern nations of the conditions which prevailed in the poetry of Rome. Greek poetry in many respects is mediaeval; the Latin poetry of the great age is Renaissance, an imitation of types derived from Greece, with quite different circumstances and a different relation of the poet to his audience.

Not that Latin or modern poetry is unsocial. It is true . . . that the tendency of modern art, including poetry, is often contrary to the popular taste of its time; the poets are often left to themselves to find their themes and elaborate their modes of expression in solitude, with results that are often found as perplexing and offensive, and as negligible, as Browning's *Sordello* was generally found to be.

What is true of the major changes in the form of poetry is, I think, true also of the change from a pre-critical to a critical age. It is true of the change from a pre-philosophical to a philosophical age; you cannot deplore criticism unless you deprecate philosophy. You may say that the development of criticism is a symptom of the development, or change, of poetry; and the development of poetry is itself a symptom of social changes. The important moment for the appearance of criticism seems to be the time when poetry ceases to be the expression of the mind of a whole people. The drama of Dryden, which furnishes the chief occasion for his critical writing, is formed by Dryden's perception that the possibilities of writing in the mode of Shakespeare were exhausted; the form persists in the tragedies of such a writer as Shirley (who is much more up to date in his comedies) after the mind and sensibility of England has altered. But Dryden was not writing plays for the whole people; he was writing in a form which had not grown out of popular tradition or popular requirements, a form the acceptance of which had therefore to come by diffusion through a small society. Something similar had been attempted by the Senecan dramatists. But the part of society to which Dryden's work, and that of the Restoration comedians, could immediately appeal constituted something like an intellectual aristocracy; when the poet finds himself in an age in which there is no intellectual aristocracy, when power is in the hands of a class so democratised that whilst still a class it represents itself to be the whole nation; when the only alternatives seem to be to talk to a coterie or to soliloquise, the difficulties of the poet and the necessity of criticism become greater. In the essay from which I have just quoted, Ker says:

There is no doubt that in the nineteenth century poets are more left to themselves than they were in the eighteenth, and the result is unmistakeable in their strength and weakness. . . . The heroic independence of Browning, and indeed all the adventurous capricious poetry of the nineteenth century, is closely related to criticism, and to the eclectic learning which ranges over the whole world in search of artistic beauty. . . . The themes are taken from all the ages and countries; the poets are eclectic students and critics, and they are justified, as explorers are justified; they sacrifice what explorers sacrifice when they leave their native home. . . . I shall not be misunderstood if I remark that their victories bring along with them some danger, if not for themselves, at least for the fashion, the tradition of poetry.

The gradual changes in the function of poetry, as society alters, will, I hope, emerge somewhat after we have considered several critics as representatives of several generations. During three hundred years criticism has come to modify its assumptions and its purposes, and it will surely continue to do so. There are several forms which criticism may take; there is always a large proportion of criticism which is retrograde or irrelevant; there are always many writers who are qualified neither by knowledge of the past nor by awareness of the sensibility and the problems of the present. Our earliest criticism, under the influence of classical studies and of Italian critics, made very large assumptions about the nature and function of literature. Poetry was a decorative art, an art for which sometimes extravagant claims were made, but an art in which the same principles seemed to hold good for every civilisation and for every society; it was an art deeply affected by the rise of a new social class, only loosely (at best) associated with the Church, a class self-conscious in its possession of the mysteries of Latin and Greek. In England the critical force due to the new contrast between Latin and vernacular met, in the sixteenth century, with just the right degree of resistance. That is to say, for the age which is represented for us by Spenser and Shakespeare, the new forces stimulated the native genius and did not overwhelm it. The purpose of my second lecture will be to give to the criticism of this period the due which it does not seem to me to have received. In the next age, the great work of Dryden in criticism is, I think, that at the right moment he became conscious of the necessity of affirming the native element in literature. Dryden is more consciously English, in his plays, than were his predecessors; his essays on the drama and on the art of translation are conscious studies of the nature of the English theatre and the English language; and even his adaptation of Chaucer is an assertion of the native tradition — rather than, what it has sometimes been taken to be, an amusing and pathetic failure to appreciate the beauty of the Chaucerian language and metric. Where the Elizabethan critics, for the most part, were aware of something to be borrowed or adapted from abroad, Dryden was aware of something to be preserved at home. But throughout this period, and for much longer, one assumption remained the same: the assumption as to what was the use of poetry. Any reader of Sidney's *Apology for Poetry* can see that his *misomousoi* against whom he defends poetry are men of straw, that he is confident of having the sympathy of his reader with him, and that he never seriously has to ask himself the questions, what poetry is for, what it does, or whether it is desirable. Sidney's assumption is that poetry gives at once delight and instruction, and is an adornment of social life and an honour to the nation.

I am very far from dissenting from these assumptions, so far as they go; my point is that for a long time they were never questioned or modified; that during that time great poetry was written, and some criticism which just because of its assumptions has permanent instruction to give. I hold indeed that in an age in which the use of poetry is something agreed upon you are more likely to get that minute and scrupulous examination of felicity and blemish, line by line, which is conspicuously absent from the criticism of our time, a criticism which seems to demand of poetry, not that it shall be well written, but that it shall be "representative of its age." I wish that we might dispose more attention to the correctness of expression, to the clarity or obscurity, to the grammatical precision or inaccuracy, to the choice of words whether just or improper, exalted or vulgar, of our verse: in short to the good or bad breeding of our poets. My point here is that a great change in the attitude towards poetry, in the expectations and demands made upon it, did come, we may say for convenience towards the end of the eighteenth century. Wordsworth and Coleridge are not merely demolishing a debased tradition, but revolting against a whole social order; and they begin to make claims for poetry which reach their highest point of exaggeration in Shelley's famous phrase, "poets are the unacknowledged legislators of mankind." Earlier laudators of poetry had said the same thing, but it did not mean the same thing; Shelley (to borrow a successful phrase from Mr. Bernard Shaw) was the first, in this tradition, of Nature's M.P.'s. If Wordsworth thought that he was simply occupied with reform of language, he was deceived; he was occupied with revolution of language; and his own language was as capable of artificiality, and no more capable of naturalness, than that of Pope — as Byron felt, and as Coleridge candidly pointed out. The decay of religion, and the attrition of political institutions, left dubious frontiers upon which the poet encroached; and the annexations of the poet were legitimised by the critic. For a long time the poet is the priest: there are still, I believe, people who imagine that they draw religious aliment from Browning or Meredith. But the next stage is best exemplified by Matthew Arnold. Arnold was too temperate and reasonable a man to maintain exactly that religious instruction is best conveyed by poetry, and he himself had very little to convey; but he discovered a new formula: poetry is not religion, but it is a capital substitute for religion — not invalid port, which may lend itself to hypocrisy, but coffee without caffeine, and tea without tannin. The doctrine of Arnold was extended, if also somewhat travestied, in the doctrine of "art for art's sake." This creed might seem a reversion to the simpler faith of an earlier time, in which the poet was like a dentist, a man with a definite job. But it was really a hopeless admission of irresponsibility. The poetry of revolt and the poetry of retreat are not of the same kind.

In our time we have moved, under various impulsions, to new positions. On the one hand the study of psychology has impelled men not only to investigate the mind of the poet with a confident ease which has led to some fantastic excesses and aberrant criticism, but also to investigate the mind of the reader and the problem of "communication" — a word which perhaps begs a question. On the other hand the study of history has shown us the relation of both form and content of poetry to the conditions of its time and place. The psychological and the sociological are probably the two best advertised varieties of modern criticism; but the number of ways in which the problems of criticism are approached was never before so great or so confusing. Never were there fewer settled assumptions as to what poetry is, or why it comes about, or what it is for. Criticism seems to have separated into several diverse kinds.

I have not made this brief review of the progress of criticism in order to lead up to associating myself with any particular tendency of modern criticism, least of all the sociological. I suggest that we may learn a good deal about criticism and about poetry by examining the history of criticism, not merely as a catalogue of successive notions about poetry, but as a process of readjustment between poetry and the world in and for which it is produced. We can learn something about poetry simply by studying what people have thought about it at one period after another; without coming to the stultifying conclusion that there is nothing to be said but that opinion changes. Second, the study of criticism, not as a sequence of random conjectures, but as readaptation, may also help us to draw some conclusions as to what is permanent or eternal in poetry, and what is merely the expression of the spirit of an age; and by discovering what does change, and how, and why, we may become able to apprehend what does not change. And by investigating the problems of what has seemed to one age and another to matter, by examining differences and identities, we may somewhat hope to extend our own limitations and liberate ourselves from some of our prejudices. I will quote at this point two passages which I may have occasion to quote again. The first is from Dryden's *Preface to Annus Mirabilis*:

The first happiness of the poet's imagination is properly invention, or the finding of the thought; the second is fancy, or the variation, deriving, or moulding of that thought, as the judgment represents it proper to the subject; the third is elocution, or the art of clothing and adorning that thought, as found and varied, in apt, significant, and sounding words; the quickness of the imagination is seen in the invention, the fertility in the fancy, and the accuracy in the expression.

The second passage is from Coleridge's *Biographia Litteraria*:

Repeated meditations led me first to suspect . . . that Fancy and Imagination were two distinct and widely different faculties, instead of being, according to the general belief, either two names with one meaning, or, at furthest, the lower and higher degree of one and the same power. It is not, I own, easy to conceive a more apposite translation of the Greek *phantasia* than the Latin *imaginatio*; but it is equally true that in all societies there exists an instinct of growth, a certain collective, unconscious good sense working progressively to desynonymise those words originally of the same meaning, which the conflux of dialects supplied to the more homogeneous languages, as the Greek and the German. . . . Milton had a highly imaginative, Cowley a very fanciful mind.[1]

The way in which the expression of the two poets and critics is determined by their respective backgrounds is very marked. Evident also is the more developed state of mind of Coleridge: his greater awareness of

---

[1] I may remark here as well as anywhere else that the statement contained in this last sentence is liable to operate an irrational persuasion upon the mind of the reader. We *agree* that Milton is a much greater poet than Cowley, and of another and superior kind. We then concede without examination that the difference may be formulated by this neat antithesis, and accept without examination the distinction between *imagination* and *fancy* which Coleridge has done no more than impose. The antithesis of *highly* against *very* is also an element of persuasion. See p. 50.

philology, and his conscious determination to make certain words mean certain things. But what we have to consider is, whether what we have here is two radically opposed theories of Poetic Imagination, or whether the two may be reconciled after we have taken account of the many causes of difference which are found in the passage of time between Dryden's generation and Coleridge's.

It may appear that most of what I have said, while it may have some bearing on the appreciation and understanding of poetry, has very little to do with the writing of it. When the critics are themselves poets, it may be suspected that they have formed their critical statements with a view to justifying their poetic practice. Such criticism as the two passages quoted is hardly designed to form the style of younger poets; it is rather, at its best, an account of the poet's experience of his own poetic activity, related in terms of his own mind. The critical mind operating *in* poetry, the critical effort which goes to the writing of it, may always be in advance of the critical mind operating *upon* poetry, whether it be one's own or someone's else. I only affirm that there is a significant relation between the best poetry and the best criticism of the same period. The age of criticism is also the age of critical poetry. And when I speak of modern poetry as being extremely critical, I mean that the contemporary poet, who is not merely a composer of graceful verses, is forced to ask himself such questions as "what is poetry for?"; not merely "what am I to say?" but rather "how and to whom am I to say it?" We have to communicate — if it is communication, for the word may beg the question — an experience which is not an experience in the ordinary sense, for it may only exist, formed out of many personal experiences ordered in some way which may be very different from the way of valuation of practical life, in the expression of it. *If* poetry is a form of "communication," yet that which is to be communicated is the poem itself, and only incidentally the experience and the thought which have gone into it. The poem's existence is somewhere between the writer and the reader; it has a reality which is not simply the reality of what the writer is trying to "express," or of his experience of writing it, or of the experience of the reader or of the writer as reader. Consequently the problem of what a poem "means" is a good deal more difficult than it at first appears. If a poem of mine entitled *Ash Wednesday* ever goes into a second edition, I have thought of prefixing to it the lines of Byron from *Don Juan*:

> Some have accused me of a strange design
>   Against the creed and morals of the land,
> And trace it in this poem every line.
>   I don't pretend that I quite understand
> My own meaning when I would be *very* fine;
>   But the fact is that I have nothing planned
> Unless it were to be a moment merry. . . .

There is some sound critical admonition in these lines. But a poem is not just either what the poet "planned" or what the reader conceives, nor is its "use" restricted wholly to what the author intended or to what it actually does for readers. Though the amount and the quality of the pleasure which any work of art has given since it came into existence is not irrelevant, still we never judge it by that; and we do not ask, after being greatly moved by the sight of a piece of architecture or the audition of a piece of music, "what has been my benefit or profit from seeing this temple or hearing this music?" In one sense the question implied by the phrase "the use of poetry" is nonsense. But there is another meaning to the question. Apart from the variety of ways in which poets have used their art, with greater or less success, with designs of instruction or persuasion, there is no doubt that a poet wishes to give pleasure, to entertain or divert people; and he should normally be glad to be able to feel that the entertainment or diversion is enjoyed by as large and various a number of people as possible. When a poet deliberately restricts his public by his choice of style of writing or of subject-matter, this is a special situation demanding explanation and extenuation, but I doubt whether this ever happens. It is one thing to write in a style which is already popular, and another to hope that one's writing may eventually become popular. From one point of view, the poet aspires to the condition of the music-hall comedian. Being incapable of altering his wares to suit a prevailing taste, if there be any, he naturally desires a state of society in which they may become popular, and in which his own talents will be put to the best use. He is accordingly vitally interested in the *use* of poetry. The subsequent lectures will treat of the varying conceptions of the use of poetry during the last three centuries, as illustrated in criticism, and especially in the criticism provided by the poets themselves.

NOTE ON THE DEVELOPMENT OF "TASTE" IN POETRY

It may be not inopportune, in connexion with some of the questions touched upon in the foregoing chapter, to summarise here certain remarks which I made elsewhere upon the Development of Taste. They are, I hope, not without some bearing upon the teaching of literature in schools and colleges.

I may be generalising my own history unwarrantably, or on the other hand I may be uttering what is already a commonplace amongst teachers and psychologists, when I put forward the conjecture that the majority of children, up to say twelve or fourteen, are capable of a certain enjoyment of poetry; that at or about puberty the majority of these find little further use for it, but that a small minority then find themselves possessed of a craving for poetry which is wholly different from any enjoyment experienced before. I do not know whether little girls have a different taste in poetry from little boys, but the responses of the latter I believe to be fairly uniform. *Horatius at the Bridge, The Burial of Sir John Moore, Bannockburn,* Tennyson's *Revenge,* some of the border ballads: a liking for martial and sanguinary poetry is no more to be discouraged than engagements with lead soldiers and pea-shooters. The only pleasure that I got from Shakespeare was the pleasure of being commended for reading him; had I been a child of more independent mind I should have refused to read him at all. Recognising the frequent deceptions of memory, I seem to remember that my early liking for the sort of verse that small boys do like vanished at about the age of twelve, leaving me for a couple of years with no sort of interest in poetry at all. I can recall clearly enough the moment when, at the age of fourteen or so, I happened to pick up a copy of Fitzgerald's *Omar* which was lying about, and the almost overwhelming introduction to a new world of feeling which this poem was the occasion of giving me. It was like a sudden conversion; the world appeared anew, painted with bright, delicious and painful colours. Thereupon I took the usual adolescent course with Byron, Shelley, Keats, Rossetti, Swinburne.

I take this period to have persisted until about my twenty-second year. Being a period of rapid assimilation, the end may not know the beginning, so different may the taste become. Like the first period of childhood, it is one beyond which I dare say many people never advance; so that such taste for poetry as they retain in later life is only a sentimental memory of the pleasures of youth, and is probably entwined with all our other sentimental retrospective feelings. It is, no doubt, a period of keen enjoyment; but we must not confuse the intensity of the poetic experience in adolescence with the intense experience of poetry. At this period, the poem, or the poetry of a single poet, invades the youthful consciousness and assumes complete possession for a time. We do not really see it as something with an existence outside ourselves; much as in our youthful experiences of love, we do not so much see the person as infer the existence of some outside object which sets in motion these new and delightful feelings in which we are absorbed. The frequent result is an outburst of scribbling which we may call imitation, so long as we are aware of the meaning of the word "imitation" which we employ. It is not deliberate choice of a poet to mimic, but writing under a kind of daemonic possession by one poet.

The third, or mature stage of enjoyment of poetry, comes when we cease to identify ourselves with the poet we happen to be reading; when our critical faculties remain awake; when we are aware of what one poet can be expected to give and what he cannot. The poem has its own existence, apart from us; it was there before us and will endure after us. It is only at this stage that the reader is prepared to distinguish between degrees of greatness in poetry; before that stage he can only be expected to distinguish between the genuine and the sham — the capacity to make this latter distinction must always be practised first. The poets we frequent in adolescence will not be arranged in any objective order of eminence, but by the personal accidents which put them into relation with us; and this is right. I doubt whether it is possible to explain to school children or even undergraduates the differences of degree among poets, and I doubt whether it is wise to try; they have not yet had enough experience of life for these matters to have much meaning. The perception of *why* Shakespeare, or Dante, or Sophocles holds the place he has is something which comes only very slowly in the course of living. And the deliberate attempt to grapple with poetry which is not naturally congenial, and some of which never will be, should be a very mature activity indeed; an activity which well repays the effort, but which cannot be recommended to young people without grave danger of deadening their sensibility to poetry and confounding the genuine *development* of taste with the sham acquisition of it.

It should be clear that the "development of *taste*" is an abstraction. To set before oneself the goal of being able to enjoy, and in the proper objective order of merit, all good poetry, is to pursue a phantom, the chase after which should be left to those whose ambition it is to be "cultivated" or "cultured," for whom art is a luxury article and its appreciation an accomplishment. For the development of genuine taste, founded on genuine feeling, is inextricable from the development of the personality and character.[1] Genuine taste is always imperfect taste — but we are all, as a matter of fact, imperfect people; and the man whose taste in poetry does not bear the stamp of his particular personality, so that there are differences in what he likes from what we like, as well as resemblances, and differences in the way of liking the same things, is apt to be a very uninteresting person with whom to discuss poetry. We may even say that to have better "taste" in poetry than belongs to one's state of development, is not to "taste" anything at all. One's taste in poetry cannot be isolated from one's

[1] In making this statement I refuse to be drawn into any discussion of the definitions of "personality" and "character."

other interests and passions; it affects them and is affected by them, and must be limited as oneself is limited.

This note is really introductory to a large and difficult question: whether the attempt to teach students to appreciate English literature should be made at all; and with what restrictions the teaching of English literature can rightly be included in any academic curriculum, if at all.

APOLOGY FOR THE
COUNTESS OF PEMBROKE

November 25th, 1932

THE literary criticism of the Elizabethan period is not very great in bulk; to the account which George Saintsbury has given there cannot in its kind be very much to add, and from his critical valuation there is not much to detract. What concerns me here is the general opinion of it which students are likely to form, in relation to the poetry of the age, on account of two "lost causes" which that criticism championed. The censure of the popular drama, and the attempt to introduce a more severe classical form illustrated by the essay of Sir Philip Sidney, and the censure of rhymed verse, and the attempt to introduce some adaptation of classical forms illustrated by the essay of Campion, might be taken, and have been taken, as striking examples of the futility of corrective criticism, and of the superiority of irreflective inspiration over calculation. If I can show that no such clear contrast is possible, and that the relation of the critical to the creative mind was not one of simple antagonism in the Elizabethan age, it will be easier for me to demonstrate the intimacy of the creative and the critical mind at a later period.

Everyone has read Campion's *Observations in the Art of English Poesie* and Daniel's *Defence of Ryme*. Campion, who except for Shakespeare was the most accomplished master of rhymed lyric of his time, was certainly in a weak position for attacking rhyme, as Daniel in his reply was not slow to observe. His treatise is known to most people merely as the repository of two very beautiful pieces, *Rose-cheeked Laura come* and *Raving war begot*, and of a number of other exercises most of which by their inferiority bear witness against him. Experimentation with semi-classical metres is less derided to-day than it was before the time of Robert Bridges. I do not believe that good English verse can be written quite in the way which Campion advocates, for it is the natural genius of the language, and not ancient authority, that must decide; better scholars than I, have suspected even that Latin versification was too much influenced by Greek models; I do not even believe that the metric of *The Testament of Beauty* is successful, and I have always preferred Dr. Bridges' earlier and more conventional verse to his later experiments. Ezra Pound's *Seafarer*, on the other hand, is a magnificent paraphrase exploiting the resources of a parent language; I discern its beneficent influence upon the work of some of the more interesting younger poets to-day. Some of the older forms of English versification are being revived to good purpose. But the point to dwell upon is not that Campion was altogether wrong, for he was not; or that he was completely downed by Daniel's rejoinder; and we must remember that in other matters Daniel was a member of the classicising school. The result of the controversy between Campion and Daniel is to establish, both that the Latin metres cannot be copied in English, and that rhyme is neither an essential nor a superfluity. Furthermore, no prosodic system ever invented can teach anyone to write good English verse. It is, as Mr. Pound has so often remarked, the musical phrase that matters.[1] The great achievement of Elizabethan versification is the development of blank verse; it is the dramatic poets, and eventually Milton, who are Spenser's true heirs. Just as Pope, who used what is nominally the same form as Dryden's couplet, bears little resemblance to Dryden, and as the writer to-day who was genuinely influenced by Pope would hardly want to use that couplet at all, so the writers who were significantly influenced by Spenser are not those who have attempted to use his stanza, which is inimitable. The second greatest accomplishment of the age was the lyric; and the lyric of Shakespeare and Campion owes its beauty not primarily to its use of rhyme or to its perfection of a "verse form," but to the fact that it is written to musical form; it is written to be sung. Shakespeare's knowledge of music is hardly likely to have been comparable to Campion's; but in that age a writer could hardly escape knowing a little. I can hardly conceive such a song as *Come Away Death* being written except in collaboration with the musician.[2] But, to return

---

[1] When Mr. Drinkwater says (*Victorian Poetry*) "there is now no new verse form to be discovered in English" it is his own conception of form that precludes novelty. He really means "there can be no new verse form exactly like the old ones" — or like what he thinks the old ones are. See a curious book on the relation of poetry to music, intended for readers with no technical knowledge of music, *Magic of Melody,* by John Murray Gibbon (Dent).

[2] The real superiority of Shakespeare's songs over Campion's is not to be found, so to speak, internally, but in their setting. I have elsewhere

to Campion and Daniel, I consider the controversy important, not because either was quite right or wrong, but because it is a part of the struggle between native and foreign elements as the result of which our greatest poetry was created. Campion pushed to an extreme a theory which he did not himself often practise; but the fact that people could then think along such lines is significant.

The essay of Sidney in which occur the passages ridiculing the contemporary stage, so frequently quoted, may have been composed as early as 1580; at any rate, was composed before the great plays of the age were written. We can hardly suppose that the writer who in passing showed not only a lively appreciation of *Chevy Chase*, but also of Chaucer, singling for mention what is Chaucer's greatest poem — *Troilus* — would have been imperceptive of the excellence of Shakespeare. But when we think of the multitude of bad plays, and the number of precious but imperfect plays, which Sidney did not live to read or see performed, we cannot deny that his lamentations have some application to the whole period. We are apt, in thinking of the age of Shakespeare, to imagine something like a fertile field in which tares and fine wheat luxuriated, in which the former could not have been eradicated without risk to the latter. Let both grow together until the harvest. I am not inclined to deny the exceptional number of writers of real poetic and dramatic genius; but I cannot help

commented upon the intense dramatic value of Shakespeare's songs at the points where they occur in the plays.

regretting that some of their best plays are no better than they are. "So falleth it out," says Sidney, "that having indeed no right Comedy, in that comical part of our Tragedy we have nothing but scurrility, unworthy of any chaste ears, or some extreme show of doltishness, indeed fit to lift up a loud laughter, and nothing else." He is perfectly right. *The Changeling* is only a solitary example in its extreme contrast between the grandeur of the main plot and the nauseousness of the secondary plot from which it has its title. The plays of Marston and Heywood — the latter a writer of some theatrical ability, the former considerably more — are similarly disfigured. In *The Witch of Edmonton* we have the odd spectacle of a play containing comic and tragic elements, each pretty certainly contributed by a different writer, each rising at moments to great heights in its own kind, but very imperfectly welded; I find the readjustments of mood required in this play very trying. Now the desire for "comic relief" on the part of an audience is, I believe, a permanent craving of human nature; but that does not mean that it is a craving that ought to be gratified. It springs from a lack of the capacity for concentration. Farce and love-romances, especially if seasoned with scabrousness, are the two forms of entertainment upon which the human mind can most easily, lovingly and for the longest time maintain its attention; but we like some farce as a relief from our sentiment, however salacious, and some sentiment as a relief from our farce, however broad. The audience which can keep its attention fixed upon *pure* tragedy or *pure* comedy is much more highly developed. The Athenian stage got relief through the chorus; and perhaps some of its tragedy may have held attention largely by its sensationalism. To my mind, Racine's *Bérénice* represents about the summit of civilisation in tragedy; and it is, in a way, a Christian tragedy, with devotion to the State substituted for devotion to divine law. The dramatic poet who can engross the reader's or the auditor's attention during the space of a *Bérénice* is the most civilised dramatist — though not necessarily the greatest, for there are other qualities to consider.

My point is this: that the Elizabethan drama did tend to approach that *unity of feeling* which Sidney desires. From the tragedy or history in which the comic element was simply left blank to be supplied by some clown favoured by the pit (as some of the farce in *Faustus* is supposed to be an abbreviation of the gags of one comedian), the drama grew to maturity, in, for example, *Coriolanus*, *Volpone*, and in a later generation *The Way of the World*. And it did this, not because docile dramatists obeyed the wishes of Sidney, but because the improvements advocated by Sidney happened to be those which a maturing civilisation would make for itself. The doctrine of *Unity of Sentiment*, in fact, happens to be right. And I think, in passing, that simply because we have been inclined to accept the "comic relief" notion as a kind of fixed law of Elizabethan drama, we have sometimes misunderstood the intention of the dramatist: as, for instance, in treating *The Jew of Malta* as a

huffe-snuffe grand tragedy disfigured by clownish ir-
relevancies of doubtful taste, we have missed its
point.

Some objectors may bring forward Shakespeare
either as a triumphant exception to this theory or as a
triumphant refutation of it. I know well how difficult
it is to fit Shakespeare into any theory, especially if
it be a theory about Shakespeare; and I cannot here
undertake a complete justification, or enter upon all
the qualifications that the theory requires. But we
start with "comic relief" as a practical necessity of
the time for the writer who had to make his living by
writing plays. What is really interesting is what
Shakespeare made of this necessity. I think that
when we turn to *Henry IV* we often feel that what we
want to re-read and linger over are the Falstaff epi-
sodes, rather than the political highfalutin of the
King's party and its adversaries. That is an error.
As we read from Part I to Part II and see Falstaff,
not merely gluttonising and playing pranks indifferent to affairs of State, but leading his band of con-
scripts and conversing with local magnates, we find
that the relief has become serious contrast, and that
political satire issues from it. In *Henry V* the two
elements are still more fused; so that we have not
merely a chronicle of kings and queens, but a universal comedy in which all the actors take part in one
event. But it is not in the histories, plays of a transient and unsatisfactory type, that we find the comic
relief most nearly taken up into a higher unity of feeling. In *Twelfth Night* and *Midsummer Night's Dream*

the farcical element is an essential to a pattern more complex and elaborate than any constructed by a dramatist before or since. The Knocking on the Gate in *Macbeth* has been cited too often for me to call attention to it; less hackneyed is the scene upon Pompey's galley in *Antony and Cleopatra*. This scene is not only in itself a prodigious piece of political satire,

> A beares the third part of the world, man...

but is a key to everything that precedes and follows. To demonstrate this point to your satisfaction would, I know, require a whole essay to itself. Here, I can only affirm that for me the violence of contrast between the tragic and the comic, the sublime and the bathetic, in the plays of Shakespeare, disappears in his maturing work; I only hope that a comparison of *The Merchant of Venice*, *Hamlet* and *The Tempest* will lead others to the same conclusion. I was once under censure for suggesting that in *Hamlet* Shakespeare was dealing with "intractable material": my words were even interpreted as maintaining that *Coriolanus* is a greater play than *Hamlet*. I am not very much interested in deciding which play of Shakespeare is greater than which other; because I am more and more interested, not in one play or another, but in Shakespeare's work as a whole. I do not think it any derogation to suggest that Shakespeare did not always succeed: such a suggestion would imply a very narrow view of success. His success must always be reckoned in understanding of what he attempted; and I believe that to admit his partial failures is to *approach* the recognition of his real greatness more closely than to hold that he was always granted plenary inspiration. I do not pretend that I think *Measure for Measure*, or *Troilus and Cressida*, or *All's Well That Ends Well*, to be a wholly "successful" play; but if any one of Shakespeare's plays were omitted we should not be able to understand the rest as well as we do. In such plays, we must consider not only the degree of unification of all the elements into a "unity of sentiment," but the quality and kind of the emotions to be unified, and the elaborateness of the pattern of unification.

This consideration may appear to have carried us far away from Sidney's simple assertion about the decorum to be observed in excluding extraneous matter; but we are really with him all the time. So much, for the present, for the Unity of Sentiment. But Sidney is orthodox in laws still more difficult to observe; for he says roundly, "the stage should represent but one place, and the uttermost time presupposed in it should be, both by Aristotle's precept and common reason, but one day." This unity of place and time is a stumbling-block so old that we think it long since worn away: a law, like some others, so universally violated, that, like the heroine of Hood,

> We thought it dying when it slept,
> And sleeping when it died.

But my point is simply that the Unities differ radically from human legislation in that they are laws of nature, and a law of nature, even when it is a law of human nature, is quite another thing from a human law. The kind of literary law in which Aristotle was interested was not law that he laid down, but law that he discovered. The laws (*not* rules) of unity of place and time remain valid in that every play which observes them *in so far as its material allows* is in that respect and degree superior to plays which observe them less. I believe that in every play in which they are not observed we only put up with their violation because we feel that something is gained which we could not have if the law *were* observed. This is not to establish another law. There *is* no other law possible. It is merely to recognise that in poetry as in life our business is to make the best of a bad job. Furthermore, we must observe that the Unities are not three separate laws. They are three aspects of one law: we may violate the law of Unity of Place more flagrantly if we preserve the law of Unity of Time, or vice versa; we may violate both if we observe more closely the law of Unity of Sentiment.

We start, most of us, with an unconscious prejudice against the Unities — I mean, we are unconscious of the large element in our feeling which is mere ignorance and mere prejudice. I mean that English-speaking peoples have immediate and intimate experience of great plays in which the Unities are grossly violated, and perhaps of inferior plays in which they are more nearly observed. Furthermore, we have a natural, inevitable and largely justifiable sympathy with the literature of our own country and language; and we have had the Unities so rubbed into us, when we studied Greek or French drama, that we may think it is because of the unfamiliar dramatic form that we do not care for them so much as we care for Shakespeare. But it is just as likely that we do not care for them because they represent the genius of an alien people and a foreign tongue, and hence are prejudiced against the dramatic form. I believe that those plays of Shakespeare which approximate more nearly to observation of the Unities are *in that respect* better plays; I would even go so far as to say that the King of Denmark, in sending Hamlet to England, was attempting to violate the Unity of Action: a crime far worse, for a man in his position, than attempted murder. And what I have denominated Unity of Sentiment is only a slightly larger term than Unity of Action.

Unity, says Butcher, in his edition of the *Poetics*, is manifested mainly in two ways:

First, in the causal connexion that binds together the several parts of a play — the thoughts, the emotions, the decisions of the will, the external events being inextricably interwoven. Secondly, in the fact that the whole series of events, with all the moral forces that are brought into collision, are directed to a single end. The action as it advances converges on a definite point. The thread of purpose running through it becomes more marked. All minor effects are subordinated to the sense of an ever-growing unity. The end is linked to the beginning with inevitable certainty, and in the end we discern the meaning of the whole.

It should be obvious that the observance of this Unity must lead us, given certain dramatic material otherwise highly valuable, inevitably to violation of

the Unities of Place and Time.[1] As for Time, Aristotle only remarks rather casually that the usual practice of tragedy was to confine itself, so far as possible,
to the action of twenty-four hours. The only modern
author who has succeeded in observing this Unity
exactly is Mr. James Joyce; and he has done so with
only slight deviation from the Unity of Place, as the
action all takes place in or near the town of Dublin,
and Dublin is a contributing cause of the unity of the
whole book. But Sir Philip Sidney, with the weight
of Italian criticism upon his back, and probably not
having read Aristotle so deeply as he had read Latin
authors and Italian critics widely, only went a little
too far: he was right in principle, and he was justified
in his strictures upon the drama of his day. A greater
critic than Sidney, the greatest critic of his time, Ben
Jonson, says wisely:

I know nothing can conduce more to letters, than to
examine the writings of the Ancients, and not to rest in
their sole authority, or take all upon trust from them; provided the plagues of judging, and pronouncing against
them, be away; such as envy, bitterness, precipitation,
impudence, and scurrile scoffing. For to all the observations of the Ancients, we have our own experience; which,
if we will use and apply, we have better means to pro-
nounce. It is true they opened the gates, and made the
way that went before us; but as guides, not commanders.

And further:

Let Aristotle and others have their dues; but if we can
make farther discoveries of truth and fitness than they,
why are we envied?

---

[1] The authority for the Unity of Place is usually held to be Castel-
vetro. It is not, of course, an Aristotelian doctrine.

It was natural that a member of the Countess of Pembroke's circle, writing while popular literature was still mostly barbarous, should be more fearful and intolerant than Ben Jonson, writing towards the end of his days, with a rich creative past in retrospect, and reviewing his own great work. I do not pretend that Sidney's criticism made any more impression upon the form which later poetic drama took than did, say, the example of Greville, Daniel or Alexander. The chief channel through which the Countess of Pembroke's circle may have affected the course of English poetry is the great civilising influence of Spenser. Spenser exercised great influence upon Marlowe; Marlowe first showed what could be done with dramatic blank verse, and Marlowe's great disciple Milton showed what could be done with blank verse in a long poem. So great the influence of Spenser seems to me, that I should say that without it we might not have had the finest developments of blank verse. Such a derivation in itself should be enough to rescue the Countess of Pembroke's friends and relatives from obscurity, enough to dignify their critical efforts, to raise them from the ignominy of wealthy well-born amateurs of the arts, or obscurantist supporters of a fastidious and sterile classicism.

So much for the two real problems of specific interest which occupied the attention of Elizabethan critics: the problem of dramatic form and the problem of verse technique. Of the fashion set by Sidney, the panegyric of poetry and the poet, I shall have more to say when I come to contrast it with the laudation of

the Poet by Shelley, and with, so to speak, his ordi-
nation by Matthew Arnold. Puttenham and Webbe
play chorus to Sidney. Poetry, we are repeatedly
told, is "making," and we are reminded that ποιεῖν
means to make. Lip-service is paid to the Aristotelian
"imitation," but none of the writers of the period
seems to have penetrated very deeply into the notion
of mimesis. The opinions of Plato and Aristotle are
garbled like a judicious advertisement selection from
a book-review. Webbe would have us believe that
Plato and Aristotle join in supposing "all wisdom and
knowledge to be included mystically in that divine in-
stinction wherewith they thought their *vates* to be inspired." The notion of divine inspiration is made the
most of. The poet expresses both divine and worldly
truth, and exerts moral influence — here "imitation"
is brought in again. Finally, the poet gives delight,
and in effect helps materially to maintain and to raise
the level of culture; no court is glorious without him,
and no people great which has no poets. Interspersed
in the discourses of Sidney, Puttenham and Webbe
are some acute observations; and Puttenham's prefa-
tory note on Speech is most interesting. I am not
concerned with these, or with the circumstances in
which these essays were brought forth; though I may
be allowed to offer a word of thanks, in passing, to
Gosson because his *School of Abuse* provoked them.
It is, however, worthy of remembrance that these critical treatises appeared just *before* the beginning of the
great age; so that if they are a sign of anything, it is
of growth and not of decay.

And in these simple effusions we have in embryo

the critical questions which were to be discussed much later. To talk of poets as makers and as inspired does not get us very far, and this notion of inspiration need not be pressed for literalness; but it shows some perception of the question: "how does the making of poetry come about?" To talk vaguely of poets as philosophers does not get us very far either, but it is the simplest reply to the question: "what is the content of poetry?" Similarly with the account of poetry in its high moral purpose, the question of the relation of art and ethics appears; and finally, in the simple assertions that poetry gives high delight and adorns society is some awareness of the problem of the relation of the poem to the reader and the place of poetry in society. Once you have started you cannot stop. And these people started before Shakespeare.

I shall have spoken to no purpose if I have given the impression that I wish simply to affirm the importance of a neglected, or rather belittled group of literary people whose taste is supposed to have been counter to that of the age. Had that been my intention I should have adopted a different scheme of treatment, dealt with them severally, and in particular have had something to say about the special importance of John Lyly in the development of English prose and of proper comedy. My purpose has been rather to determine the relation of the critical currents to the general stream of creative activity. In that form of historical survey which is not concerned with the total movement of literature, but with — on the lowest level — mere readability, and which aims to tell us what works we can still enjoy, which emphasises those books which men have found it worth their while to continue to read and which are valuable to us irrespective of their historical position, some of these writers are properly ignored. The works of Sir Philip Sidney, excepting a few sonnets, are not among those to which one can return for perpetual refreshment; the *Arcadia* is a monument of dulness. But I have wished to affirm that in looking at the period with an interest in the development of the critical consciousness in and towards poetry, you cannot dissociate one group of people from another; you cannot draw a line and say here is backwater, here is the main stream. In the drama, we seem to have on the one hand almost the whole body of men of letters, a crowd of scholars coming down from Oxford and Cambridge to pick a poor living in London, needy and often almost desperate men of talent; and on the other an alert, curious, semi-barbarous public, fond of beer and bawdry, including much the same sort of people whom one encounters in the local outlying theatres to-day, craving cheap amusement to thrill their emotions, arouse their mirth and satisfy their curiosity; and between the entertainers and the entertained a fundamental homogeneity of race, of sense of humour and sense of right and wrong. The worst fault that poetry can commit is to be dull; and the Elizabethan dramatists were more or less frequently saved from dulness or galvanised into animation by the necessity to amuse. Their livelihood depended upon it: they had to amuse or starve.

THE AGE OF DRYDEN

December 2nd, 1932

IN MY previous lecture I was concerned with the Elizabethan critical mind expressing itself before the greater part of the great literature of the age had been written. Between them and Dryden occurs one great critical mind, that of a great poet whose critical writing appears to belong to quite the end of the period. If I treated Ben Jonson's opinions with complete respect, I should condemn myself for speaking or writing at all; for he says roundly, "to judge of poets is only the faculty of poets; and not of all poets, but the best." Nevertheless, though I am not a good enough poet to judge of Jonson, I have already tried to do so, and cannot now make matters worse. Between Sidney and Campion in the latter part of the sixteenth century, and Jonson writing towards the end of his life, the greatest period of English poetry is comprehended; and the maturing of the English mind in this time is well seen by reading the treatises of Sidney and his contemporaries, and then the *Discoveries* of Jonson. He called his *Discoveries* also *Timber*, and it is timber with much undergrowth and dead wood in it, but also living trees. In some places, Jonson does but express in a more adult style the same commonplaces. About poetry:

The study of it (if we will trust Aristotle) offers to mankind a certain rule, and pattern of living well, and happily; disposing us to all civil offices of society. If we will believe

Tully, it nourisheth, and instructeth, our youth; delights
our age; adorns our prosperity; comforts our adversity;
entertains us at home; keeps us company abroad, travails
with us; watches, divides the time of our earnest, and
sports; shares in our country recesses, and recreations;
insomuch as the wisest and best learned have thought her
the absolute mistress of manners, and nearest of kin to
virtue.

This list of the merits of poetry, with its conditional
references to Aristotle and Tully, has the quaintness
of a generation near to Montaigne, and is no more
convincing than a patent medicine circular; and it
has some of the heavy sententiousness of Francis
Bacon. Secondary to the serious advantages to be derived from poetry, comes the assurance that poetry
gives pleasure, or, as he says, guides us by the hand of
action, with a ravishing delight, and incredible sweet-
ness. The questions implied are, as I said towards the
end of my last lecture, among those fundamental to
criticism: Jonson has put them in a riper style than
that of the critics who wrote in his youth, but he has
not advanced the enquiry. The authority of antiquity, and the assent of our prejudices, are enough. It
is rather in his practical criticism — I mean here not
so much his criticism of individual writers, but his
advice to the practitioner, that Jonson has made
progress. He requires in the poet, first, "a goodness
of natural wit." "To this perfection of nature in our
poet, we require exercise of those parts, and frequent." His third requisite in a poet pleases me expe-
cially: "the third requisite in our poet, or maker, is
Imitation, to be able to convert the substances, or

riches of another poet, to his own use." When we come to a passage beginning "In writing there is to be regarded the Invention, and the Fashion" we may, if we have already read some later critics, expect more than we get. For so far as I understand him Jonson means nothing more than that before you write you must have something to write about; which is a manifest truth frequently ignored both by those who are trying to learn to write and by some of those who endeavour to teach writing. But when we compare such passages as these from Jonson with the passage which I quoted from Dryden in my first lecture, we feel that in Dryden we meet for the first time a man who is speaking to *us*. It is from a critical essay written before Dryden had really found out how to write poetry; but it is something very different from an appeal to the ancients; it is really analytical. I will presume to quote it again for the purpose of closer examination:

The first happiness of the poet's imagination is properly invention, or the finding of the thought; the second is fancy, or the variation, deriving, or moulding of that thought, as the judgement represents it proper to the subject; the third is elocution, or the art of clothing and adorning that thought, as found and varied, in apt, significant, and sounding words; the quickness of the imagination is seen in the invention, the fertility in the fancy, and the accuracy in the expression.

"Finding of the thought" does not mean finding a copy-book maxim, or starting with a synopsis of what we are going to put into verse, finding an "idea" which is later to be "clothed and adorned" in a rather

literal interpretation of the metaphor. It corresponds
to the inception of any piece of imaginative writing.
It is not casting about for a subject, upon which, when
found, the "imagination" is to be exercised; for we
must remark that "invention" is the first moment in a
process only the *whole* of which Dryden calls "imagination," and no less than the whole of which corresponds to the celebrated and admirable account of
imagination given by Shakespeare in *Midsummer
Night's Dream*. "Invention" in the sense used here
by Dryden does not seem to me to be properly cov-
ered by the *New English Dictionary*, which quotes
this very passage in support of the following definition: "The devising of a subject, idea, or method of
treatment, by exercise of the intellect or imagination." The words "intellect or imagination" strike
me as a burking of the question: if there is a clear distinction between invention by exercise of intellect and
invention by exercise of imagination, then two definitions are called for; and if there is no difference between intellectual and imaginative invention there
can hardly be much difference between imagination
and intellect. But Dryden is talking expressly about
imagination, not about intellect. Furthermore, the
word "devising" suggests the deliberate putting together out of materials at hand; whereas I believe that
Dryden's "invention" includes the sudden irruption
of the germ of a new poem, possibly merely as a state
of feeling. His "invention" is surely a finding, a
trouvaille. "Fancy" represents the conscious elabora-
tion of the original *donnée* — I prefer not to call that

which is found by invention by the name of "idea";
and fancy, I believe, covers also the conscious and deliberate uniting of several inventions in one poem.
"Variation, deriving, or moulding of that thought,"
Dryden calls it. "Variation" and "moulding" are, I
think, pretty clear; "deriving" is more difficult. I
think that the definition 3B in the *N.E.D.* comes
pretty close to it: "To extend by branches or modifi-
cations." Fancy is an activity of the imagination
rather than of the intellect, but is necessarily in part
an intellectual activity, inasmuch as it is a "moulding
of the thought as judgement represents it proper."
Dryden does not, I believe, necessarily imply that the
"third happiness" of poetic imagination, "elocution," is a third *act*; I mean, that the act of finding the
proper words, "clothing and adorning" the thought,
begins only after the operation of fancy is complete.
In fancy the finding of the words seems to me already
to have begun; that is, fancy is partly verbal; nevertheless, the work of elocution, "clothing and adorning
in apt, significant and sounding words," is the last to
be completed. Observe that "sounding" here means
what we, just as approximately, should be likely to
call "musical": the finding of the words and the order
of words expressive of the underlying mood which belongs to the invention. (Shakespeare's great line in
King Lear,

Never, never, never, never, never,

is just as *sounding* as Poe's line admired by Ernest
Dowson,

The viol, the violet and the vine.)

We are liable, I think, to underrate Dryden's critical
analyses, by assuming that they only apply to the
kind of poetry that he writes himself; and thus we
may overlook his meaning, as of the word "invention." Even if Dryden's poetry seems to us of a peculiar, and, as it has seemed to many, a peculiarly
unpoetic type, we need not conclude that his mind
operated quite differently from those of poets at other
periods; and we must remember his catholic and discriminating taste in poetry.

I do not need, I think, to quote again here the passage from Coleridge which I quoted in contrast to that
of Dryden, because I do not propose to examine it so
narrowly. You will have observed the more developed
etymological sense. I am not sure that Coleridge has
made as satisfactory an analysis as that of Dryden.
The distinction is too simple. The last sentence,
"Milton had a highly imaginative, Cowley a very
fanciful mind," should be enough to arouse suspicion.
It represents a course of argument which is specious.
You assert a distinction, you select two authors who
illustrate it to your satisfaction, and you ignore the
negative instances or difficult cases. If Coleridge had
written, "Spenser had a highly imaginative, Donne a
very fanciful mind," the assumed superiority of imagination to fancy might not appear quite so immediately convincing. Not only Cowley, but all the metaphysical poets, had very fanciful minds, and if you
removed the fancy and left only imagination, as Coleridge appears to use these terms, you would have no
metaphysical poetry. The distinction is admittedly

a distinction of value; the term "fancy" is really
made derogatory, just applicable to clever verse that
you do not like.

Between Dryden, and Wordsworth and Coleridge
the one great critical mind is that of Johnson. After
Dryden, and before Johnson, there is much just criticism, but no great critic. The inferiority of common
minds to great is more painfully apparent in those
modest exercises of the mind in which common sense
and sensibility are needed, than in their failure to
ascend to the higher flights of genius. Addison is a
conspicuous example of this embarrassing mediocrity,
and he is a symptom of the age which he announced.
The difference between the temper of the eighteenth
century and that of the seventeenth is profound.
Here, for example, is Addison on the subject on which
we have already heard Dryden and Coleridge, the
Imagination:

There are few words in the English language which are
employed in a more loose and uncircumscribed sense than
those of the fancy and the imagination. I therefore thought
it necessary to fix and determine the notion of these two
words, as I intend to make use of them in the thread of my
following speculations, that the reader may conceive rightly
what is the subject which I proceed upon.[1]

It is perhaps as well to warn you that Addison is a
writer towards whom I feel something very like an-
tipathy. It seems to me that even in these few words
the smugness and priggishness of the man appear.

[1] *The Spectator*, June 21st, 1712, No. 411.

Of an age during which the Church sank to an unloveliness unequalled before or since, Addison was one of the most apposite ornaments; he possessed the Christian virtues, and all in the wrong order: humility was the least of his attainments. It would seem, from this account of "fancy" and "imagination," that Addison had never read, certainly never pondered, Dryden's remarks upon the subject. I do not feel sure, however, that this yoking of fancy and imagination by Addison did not strike the eye of Coleridge, and start him upon his process of differentiation. For Dryden "imagination" was the whole process of poetic creation in which fancy was one element. Addison starts out to "fix and determine" the notion of the two words; I cannot find any fixing or determining of the word "fancy" in this or the following essays on the subject; he is entirely occupied with the imagination, and primarily with the visual imagination, and solely with the visual imagination according to Mr. Locke. That is a debt which he hastens to acknowledge: he pays a handsome testimonial to the scientific truths which Locke has established. Alas, philosophy is not science, nor is literary criticism; and it is an elementary error to think that we have discovered as objective laws what we have merely imposed by private legislation.

It is curious to find the old notions of delight and instruction, with which the sixteenth century defended poetry, cropping up again in a form typical of the age of Addison, but hardly with any greater profundity of meaning. Addison observes:

A man of a polite imagination is let into a great many pleasures that the vulgar are not capable of receiving. He can converse with a picture, and find an agreeable companion in a statue. He meets with a secret refreshment in a description, and often finds a greater satisfaction in the prospect of fields and meadows, than another does in the possession.

The eighteenth-century emphases are illuminating. Instead of the courtier, we have the man of polite imagination. I suppose that Addison is what one would describe as a gentleman; as one might say, no better than a gentleman. His notion of recommending imagination, because it enables you to enjoy a statue or a piece of property without having to put your hand in your pocket to pay for it, is a very happy thought indeed. And gentleman as he is, he has a very low opinion of those who are not genteel:

There are indeed but very few who know how to be idle and innocent, or have a relish of any pleasures that are not criminal.

Tell that, we might add, to the Unemployed. The particular examination of Addison may be left to Mr. Saintsbury, whose *History of Criticism* is always delightful, generally useful, and most often right. My introduction of Addison has not been, however, merely in order to poke fun at him. What is interesting and relevant to observe in Addison is not merely deterioration, a deterioration of society, but of interesting change. In the same series of papers on Imagination he says:

It may here be worth our while to examine how it comes to pass that several readers, who are all acquainted with the same language, and know the meaning of the words they read, should nevertheless have a different relish of the same descriptions.

Addison does not succeed in following up this very important question with any very important answer, but it is suggestive as the first awareness of the problem of communication; and his whole discussion of the nature of imagination, however fruitless for the purposes of literary criticism, is a very interesting attempt at a general aesthetics. Any matter which comes eventually to be the subject of detailed investigation and specialised labour may be preceded, long before any fruitful development takes place, by such random guesses as these, which though not directly productive of fruitful results indicate the direction in which the mind is moving.

Addison, although too poor a poet to be strictly comparable to the other critics whom I have mentioned and have to mention, acquires importance by being thoroughly representative of his age. The history of every branch of intellectual activity provides the same record of the diminution of England from the time of Queen Anne. It is not so much the intellect, but something superior to intellect, which went for a long time into eclipse; and this luminary, by whatever name we may call it, has not yet wholly issued from its secular obnubilation. The age of Dryden was still a great age, though beginning to suffer a death of the spirit, as the coarsening of its verse-rhythms shows; by the time of Addison theology, devotion and poetry fell fast into a formalistic slumber.

Addison is definitely a writer for a middle class, a bourgeois literary dictator. He was a popular lecturer. To him poetry meant delight and edification in a new way. Johnson has here, in his own language, fixed admirably the difference between Dryden and Addison as directors of taste:

Dryden has, not many years before, scattered criticism over his prefaces with very little parsimony; but though he sometimes condescended to be somewhat familiar, his manner was in general too scholastic for those who had yet their rudiments to learn, and found it not easy to understand their master. His observations were framed rather for those that were learning to write, than for those that read only to talk.

An instructor like Addison was now wanting, whose remarks, being superficial, might be easily understood, and being just, might prepare the mind for more attainments. Had he presented *Paradise Lost* to the public with all the pomp of system and severity of science, the criticism would perhaps have been admired, and the poem still have been neglected; but by the blandishments of gentleness and facility he has made Milton an universal favourite, with whom readers of every class think it necessary to be pleased.

It was still then, apparently, a not unlettered period, in which readers of *any* class could think it necessary to be pleased with *Paradise Lost*. But the usual classification of Dryden, Addison and Johnson together as critics of an Augustan age fails to allow adequately for two differences: the spiritual deterioration in society between the periods of the first two, and the remarkable isolation of the third. It is surely by unconscious irony that we speak of an "age of

Johnson" as we do of an "age of Dryden" or an "age of Addison." Lonely in his life, Johnson seems to me still more lonely in his intellectual and moral existence. He could not even very much *like* the poetry of his age with which admirers of the eighteenth century now "think it necessary to be pleased"; if more than just to Collins, he was no more than severe to Gray. He himself, I am convinced, is their superior as a poet, not in sensibility, not in metrical dexterity or aptness of phrase, but in a moral elevation just short of sublimity.

Such writing as Johnson's *Lives of the Poets* and his essay on Shakespeare loses none of its permanence from the consideration that every generation must make its own appraisal of the poetry of the past, in the light of the performance of its contemporaries and immediate predecessors. Criticism of poetry moves between two extremes. On the one hand the critic may busy himself so much with the implications of a poem, or of one poet's work — implications moral, social, religious or other — that the poetry becomes hardly more than a text for a discourse. Such is the tendency of the moralising critics of the nineteenth century, to which Landor makes a notable exception. Or if you stick too closely to the "poetry" and adopt no attitude towards what the poet has to say, you will tend to evacuate it of all significance. And furthermore there is a philosophic borderline, which you must not transgress too far or too often, if you wish to preserve your standing as a critic, and are not prepared to present yourself as a philosopher, metaphysician, sociologist, or psychologist instead. Johnson, in these respects, is a type of critical integrity. Within his limitations, he is one of the great critics; and he is a great critic partly because he keeps within his limitations. When you know what they are, you know where you are. Considering all the temptations to which one is exposed in judging contemporary writing, all the prejudices which one is tempted to indulge in judging writers of the immediately preceding generation, I view Johnson's *Lives of the Poets* as a masterpiece of the judicial bench. His style is not so formally perfect as that of some other prose writers of his time. It reads often like the writing of a man who is more habituated to talking than to writing; he seems to think aloud, and in short breaths, rather than in the long periods of the historian or the orator. His criticism is as salutary against the dogmatic excesses of the eighteenth century — more indulged in France than in England — as it is against excessive adulation of individual poets with their faults as well as virtues. We shall have, in the nineteenth century, several vagaries to contemplate, of critics who do not so much practise criticism as make use of it for other purposes. For Johnson poetry was still poetry, and not another thing. Had he lived a generation later, he would have been obliged to look more deeply into the foundations, and so would have been unable to leave us an example of what criticism ought to be for a civilisation which, being settled, has no need, while it lasts, to enquire into the functions of its parts.

WORDSWORTH AND COLERIDGE

IT IS natural, and in so rapid and superficial a review as this inevitable, to consider the criticism of Wordsworth and of Coleridge together. But we must keep in mind how very different were not only the men themselves, but the circumstances and motives of the composition of their principal critical statements. Wordsworth's *Preface to Lyrical Ballads* was written while he was still in his youth, and while his poetic genius still had much to do; Coleridge wrote the *Biographia Litteraria* much later in life, when poetry, except for that one brief and touching lament for lost youth, had deserted him, and when the disastrous effects of long dissipation and stupefaction of his powers in transcendental metaphysics were bringing him to a state of lethargy. With the relation of Coleridge's thought to subsequent theological and political development I am not here concerned. The *Biographia* is our principal document; and in connexion with that there is one piece of his formal verse which in its passionate self-revelation rises almost to the height of great poetry. I mean *Dejection: an Ode*.

> There was a time when, though my path was rough,
> This joy within me dallied with distress,
> And all misfortunes were but as the stuff
> Whence Fancy made me dream of happiness:
> For hope grew round me, like the twining vine,
> And fruits and foliage, not my own, seemed mine.

But now affliction bows me down to earth:
Nor care I that they rob me of my mirth;
     But oh! each visitation
Suspends what nature gave me at my birth,
    My shaping spirit of imagination.
For not to think of what I needs must feel,
    But to be still and patient, all I can;
And haply by abstruse research to steal
    From my own nature all the natural man —
    This was my sole resource, my only plan:
Till that which suits a part infects the whole,
And now is almost grown the habit of my soul.

This ode was written by April 4th, 1802: the *Biographia Litteraria* were not published for fifteen years after that. The lines strike my ear as one of the saddest of confessions that I have ever read. When I spoke of Coleridge as drugging himself with metaphysics I was thinking seriously of these his own words: "haply by abstruse research to steal from my own nature all the natural man." Coleridge was one of those unhappy persons — Donne, I suspect, was such another — of whom one might say, that if they had not been poets, they might have made something of their lives, might even have had a career; or conversely, that if they had not been interested in so many things, crossed by such diverse passions, they might have been great poets. It was better for Coleridge, as poet, to read books of travel and exploration than to read books of metaphysics and political economy. He did genuinely want to read books of metaphysics and political economy, for he had a certain talent for such subjects. But for a few years he had been visited by the Muse (I know of no poet to whom this hackneyed metaphor is better applicable) and thenceforth was a haunted man; for anyone who has ever been visited by the Muse is thenceforth haunted. He had no vocation for the religious life, for there again somebody like a Muse, or a much higher being, is to be invoked; he was condemned to know that the little poetry he had written was worth more than all he could do with the rest of his life. The author of *Biographia Litteraria* was already a ruined man. Sometimes, however, to be a "ruined man" is itself a vocation.

Wordsworth, on the other hand, wrote his *Preface*, as I have said, while in the plenitude of his poetic powers and while his reputation was still only sustained by readers of discernment. And he was of an opposite poetic type to Coleridge. Whether the bulk of his genuine poetic achievement is so much greater than Coleridge's as it appears, is uncertain. Whether his power and inspiration remained with him to the end is, alas, not even doubtful. But Wordsworth had no ghastly shadows at his back, no Eumenides to pursue him; or if he did, he gave no sign and took no notice; and he went droning on the still sad music of infirmity to the verge of the grave. His inspiration never having been of that sudden, fitful and terrifying kind that visited Coleridge, he was never, apparently, troubled by the consciousness of having lost it. As André Gide's Prometheus said, in the lecture which he gave before a large audience in Paris: "*Il faut avoir un aigle.*" Coleridge remained in contact with his eagle. Neither in detail of life and interest were the two men similar — Wordsworth indifferent to books, Coleridge the voracious reader. But they had that in common which was more important than all differences: they were the two most original poetic minds of their generation. Their influence upon each other was considerable; though probably the influence of Wordsworth upon Coleridge, during their brief period of intimate association, was greater than that of Coleridge upon Wordsworth. This reciprocal influence would hardly have been possible to such a degree without another influence which held the two men together, and affected both of them more deeply than either knew, the influence of a great woman. No woman has ever played so important a part in the lives of two poets at once — I mean their poetic lives — as did Dorothy Wordsworth.

The emphasis upon the differences of mind, temperament and character of the two men must be all the greater because their critical statements must be read together. In some respects there is of course, as would be expected, a conscious difference of opinion. Wordsworth wrote his *Preface* to defend his own manner of writing poetry, and Coleridge wrote the *Biographia* to defend Wordsworth's poetry; or in part he did. I must confine myself to two points. One is Coleridge's doctrine of fancy and imagination; the other is that on which Coleridge and Wordsworth made common cause: their new theory of poetic diction.

Let me take up the latter point first. In this matter of poetic diction, it is at first very hard to understand what all the fuss is about. Wordsworth's poems had met with no worse reception than verse of such novelty is accustomed to receive. I myself can remember a time when some question of "poetic diction" was in the air; when Ezra Pound issued his statement that "poetry ought to be as well written as prose"; and when he and I and our colleagues were mentioned by a writer in *The Morning Post* as "literary bolsheviks" and by Mr. Arthur Waugh (with a point which has always escaped me) as "drunken helots." But I think that we believed that we were affirming forgotten standards, rather than setting up new idols. Wordsworth, when he said that his purpose was "to imitate, and as far as possible, to adopt, the very language of men," was only saying in other words what Dryden had said, and fighting the battle which Dryden had fought; and Mr. Garrod, in calling attention to this fact, seems to me intemperate in asserting that Dryden had never made real to himself "two vital considerations: first, that such language must express passion, and secondly, that it must base itself in just observation." Dryden among the shades might meditate upon Mr. Garrod's conception of passion and observation. And on the other hand, as has also been pointed out, first by Coleridge himself in the *Biographia*, Wordsworth by no means worried himself to excess in observing his own principles. "The language of the middle and lower classes of society"[1] is of course perfectly proper when you are representing

[1] What was Wordsworth's conception of the language of the upper classes of society?

dramatically the *speech* of these classes, and then no other language is proper; similarly when you are representing dramatically the language of the upper classes; but on other occasions, it is not the business of the poet to talk like *any* class of society, but like himself — rather better, we hope, than any actual class; though when any class of society happens to have the best word, phrase or expletive for anything, then the poet is entitled to it. As for the current style of writing when the *Lyrical Ballads* appeared, it was what any style of writing becomes when it falls into the hands of people who cannot even be called mediocrities. True, Gray was overrated: but then Johnson had come down on Gray with a deadlier force than Wordsworth could exert. And Donne has seemed to us, in recent years, as striking a peculiarly conversational style; but did Wordsworth or Coleridge acclaim Donne? No, when it came to Donne — and Cowley — you will find that Wordsworth and Coleridge were led by the nose by Samuel Johnson; they were just as eighteenth century as anybody; except that where the eighteenth century spoke of lack of elegance, the Lake poets found lack of passion. And much of the poetry of Wordsworth and Coleridge is just as turgid and artificial and elegant as any eighteenth-century die-hard could wish. What then was all the fuss about?

There really was something to make a fuss about. I do not know whether Professor Garrod has grasped it, but if so he seems to ignore it; Professor Harper,[1]

[1] In his Life of Wordsworth.

however, seems to have it by the right lug. There is a remarkable letter of Wordsworth's in 1801 which he wrote to Charles James Fox in sending him a copy of the *Ballads*. You will find a long extract from this letter in Professor Harper's book. I quote one sentence. In commending his poems to the fashionable politician's attention Wordsworth says:

Recently by the spreading of manufactures through every part of the country, by the heavy taxes upon postage, by workhouses, houses of industry, and the invention of soup shops, etc., superadded to the increasing disproportion between the price of labour and that of the necessaries of life, the bonds of domestic feeling among the poor, as far as the influence of these things has extended, have been weakened, and in innumerable instances entirely destroyed.

Wordsworth then proceeds to expound a doctrine which nowadays is called distributism. And Wordsworth was not merely taking advantage of an opportunity to lecture a rather disreputable statesman and rouse him to useful activity; he was seriously explaining the content and purpose of his poems: without this preamble Mr. Fox could hardly be expected to make head or tail of the Idiot Boy or the sailor's parrot. You may say that this public spirit is irrelevant to Wordsworth's greatest poems; nevertheless I believe that you will understand a great poem like *Resolution and Independence* better if you understand the purposes and social passions which animated its author; and unless you understand these you will misread Wordsworth's literary criticism entirely. Incidentally, those who speak of Wordsworth as the original Lost Leader (a reference which Browning, as I remember, denied) should make pause and consider that when a man takes politics and social affairs seriously the difference between revolution and reaction may be by the breadth of a hair, and that Wordsworth may possibly have been no renegade but a man who thought, so far as he thought at all, for himself. But it is Wordsworth's social interest that inspires his own novelty of form in verse, and backs up his explicit remarks upon poetic diction; and it is really this social interest which (consciously or not) the fuss was all about. It was not so much from lack of thought as from warmth of feeling that Wordsworth originally wrote the words "the language of conversation in middle and lower class society." It was not from any recantation of political principles, but from having had it brought to his attention that, as a general literary principle, this would never do, that he altered them. Where he wrote "my purpose was to imitate, and as far as possible, to adopt, the very language of men" he was saying what no serious critic could disapprove.

Except on this point of diction, and that of "choosing incidents from common life," Wordsworth is a most orthodox critic. It is true that he uses the word "enthusiasm" which the eighteenth century did not like, but in the matter of mimesis he is more deeply Aristotelian than some who have aimed at following Aristotle more closely. He says of the poet:

To these qualities he has added a disposition to be affected more than other men by absent things as if they were present; an ability of conjuring up in himself passions, which are indeed far from being the same as those produced by real events, yet (especially in those parts of the general sympathy which are pleasing and delightful) do more nearly resemble the passions produced by real events, than anything which, from the motions of their own minds merely, other men are accustomed to feel in themselves.

Here is the new version of Imitation, and I think that it is the best so far.

Aristotle, I have been told, has said, that Poetry is the most philosophic of all writing; it is so: its object is truth, not individual and local, but general, and operative.

I find that "it is so" very exhilarating. For my part, rather than be parrotted by a hundred generations, I had rather be neglected and have one man eventually come to my conclusions and say "there is an old author who found this out before I did."

When you find Wordsworth as the seer and prophet whose function it is to instruct and edify through pleasure, as if this were something he had found out for himself, you may begin to think that there is something in it, at least for some kinds of poetry. Some portions of this enthusiasm I believe Wordsworth communicated to Coleridge. But Wordsworth's revolutionary faith was more vital to him than it was to Coleridge. You cannot say that it inspired his revolution in poetry, but it cannot be disentangled from the motives of his poetry. Any radical change in poetic form is likely to be the symptom of some very much deeper change in society and in the individual. I doubt whether the impulse in Coleridge would have been strong enough to have worked its way out, but for the example and encouragement of Wordsworth. I would not be understood as affirming that revolutionary enthusiasm is the best parent for poetry, or as justifying revolution on the ground that it will lead to an outburst of poetry — which would be a wasteful, and hardly justifiable way of producing poetry. Nor am I indulging in sociological criticism, which has to suppress so much of the data, and which is ignorant of so much of the rest. I only affirm that all human affairs are involved with each other, that consequently all history involves abstraction, and that in attempting to win a full understanding of the poetry of a period you are led to the consideration of subjects which at first sight appear to have little bearing upon poetry. These subjects have accordingly a good deal to do with the criticism of poetry; and it is such subjects which make intelligible Wordsworth's inability to appreciate Pope, and the irrelevance of the metaphysical poets to the interest which he and Coleridge had at heart.

With the foregoing observations in mind, let me turn to consider the great importance, in the *Biographia Litteraria*, of the distinction between Fancy and Imagination already touched upon, and of the definition of Imagination given in a later passage. "Repeated meditations led me first to suspect . . . that Fancy and Imagination were two distinct and widely different faculties, instead of being, according

to the general belief, either two names with one meaning, or, at furthest, the lower and higher degrees of
one and the same power." In Chapter XIII he draws
the following important distinctions.

The Imagination then I consider either as primary, or
secondary. The Primary Imagination I hold to be the
living power and prime agent of all human perception, and
as a repetition in the finite mind of the eternal act of creation in the infinite I AM. The Secondary Imagination I
consider as an echo of the former, co-existing with the conscious will, yet still as identical with the primary in the
kind of its agency, and differing only in *degree*, and in the
mode of its operation. It dissolves, diffuses, dissipates, in
order to re-create; or where this process is rendered impossible, yet still at all events it struggles to idealise and to
unify. It is essentially *vital*, even as all objects (*as* objects)
are essentially fixed and dead.

FANCY, on the other hand, has no other counters to
play with, but fixities and definites. The fancy is indeed no
other than a mode of memory emancipated from the order
of time and space; while it is blended with, and modified
by that empirical phenomenon of the will, which we express by the word Choice. But equally with the ordinary
memory the Fancy must receive all its materials ready
made from the law of association.

I have read some of Hegel and Fichte, as well as
Hartley (who turns up at any moment with Coleridge), and forgotten it; of Schelling I am entirely ignorant at first hand, and he is one of those numerous
authors whom, the longer you leave them unread, the
less desire you have to read. Hence it may be that I
wholly fail to appreciate this passage. My mind is
too heavy and concrete for any flight of abstruse

reasoning. If, as I have already suggested, the difference between imagination and fancy amounts in practice to no more than the difference between good and bad poetry, have we done more than take a turn round Robin Hood's barn? It is only if fancy can be an ingredient in good poetry, and if you can show some good poetry which is the better for it; it is only if the distinction illuminates our immediate preference of one poet over another, that it can be of use to a practical mind like mine. Fancy may be "no other than a mode of memory emancipated from the order of space and time"; but it seems unwise to talk of memory in connexion with fancy and omit it altogether from the account of imagination. As we have learnt from Dr. Lowes's *Road to Xanadu* (if we did not know it already) memory plays a very great part in imagination, and of course a much larger part than can be proved by that book; Professor Lowes had only literary reminiscences to deal with, and they are the only kind of reminiscence which can be fully traced and identified: but how much more of memory enters into creation than only our reading! Mr. Lowes has, I think, demonstrated the importance of instinctive and unconscious, as well as deliberate selection. Coleridge's taste, at one period of life, led him first to read voraciously in a certain type of book, and then to select and store up certain kinds of imagery from those books.[1] And I should say that the mind of any

---

[1] And by a right appreciation. The circumstances of early exploration might well stimulate the imaginations of those who endeavoured to set down precisely what they had seen in such a way as to convey an accurate

poet would be magnetised in its own way, to select automatically, in his reading (from picture papers and cheap novels, indeed, as well as serious books, and least likely from works of an abstract nature, though even these are aliment for some poetic minds), the material — an image, a phrase, a word — which may be of use to him later. And this selection probably runs through the whole of his sensitive life. There might be the experience of a child of ten, a small boy peering through sea-water in a rock-pool, and finding a sea-anemone for the first time: the simple experience (not so simple, for an exceptional child, as it looks) might lie dormant in his mind for twenty years, and re-appear transformed in some verse-context charged with great imaginative pressure. There is so much memory in imagination that if you are to distinguish between imagination and fancy in Coleridge's way you must define the difference between memory in imagination and memory in fancy; and it is not enough to say that the one "dissolves, diffuses and dissipates" the memories in order to re-create, whilst the other deals with "fixities and definites." This distinction, in itself, need not give you distinct imagination and fancy, but only degrees of imaginative success. It would seem from Mr. Richards's note [1] that he is almost as much baffled by the passage which I have quoted, or at least by part

impression to Europeans who had no experience of anything similar. They would often, naturally, stimulate the imagination beyond the perception, but it is usually the accurate images, the fidelity of which may still be recognised, that are the most telling.

[1] *Principles of Literary Criticism*, p. 191.

of it, as I am. You have to forget all about Coleridge's fancy to learn anything from him about imagination — as with Addison — but from Coleridge there is a good deal to learn. I quote another passage, in the form in which Mr. Richards has abbreviated it:

That synthetic and magical power, to which we have exclusively appropriated the name of imagination . . . reveals itself in the balance or reconciliation of opposite or discordant qualities . . . the sense of novelty and freshness, with old and familiar objects; a more than usual state of emotion, with more than usual order; judgement ever awake and steady self-possession with enthusiasm and feeling profound or vehement." "The sense of musical delight . . . with the power of reducing multitude into variety of effect, and modifying a series of thoughts by some one predominant thought or feeling."

What such descriptions are worth, from the point of view of psychological criticism of to-day, can best be learnt from Mr. Richards's book from which I have quoted them. What is my concern here is a less profound matter, the place of Wordsworth and Coleridge in the historical process of criticism. You will have observed in the passage just quoted a richness and depth, an awareness of complication which takes it far out of the range of Dryden. This is not simply because Coleridge thought more profoundly than Dryden, though he did. Nor am I sure that Coleridge learned so much from German philosophers, or earlier from Hartley, as he thought he did; what is best in his criticism seems to come from his own delicacy and subtlety of insight as he reflected upon his own experience of writing poetry. Of the two poets as critics, it was Wordsworth who knew better what he was about: his critical insight, in this one *Preface* and the *Supplement*, is enough to give him the highest place. I do not assign him this position because he cared about the revival of agriculture and the relation of production and consumption, though such interests are symptomatic; there is, in his poetry and in his *Preface*, a profound spiritual revival, an inspiration communicated rather to Pusey and Newman, to Ruskin, and to the great humanitarians, than to the accredited poets of the next age. Coleridge, with his authority due to his great reading, probably did much more than Wordsworth to bring attention to the profundity of the philosophic problems into which the study of poetry may take us. And the two men together need no third with them to illustrate the mind of an age of conscious change. It is not merely that they were interested in a variety of speculative subjects and of practical matters of importance for their time, but that their interests were involved in each other: and the first faint sign of such complication appeared when Addison derived his theory of imagination in the arts from the theories of Locke. In Wordsworth and Coleridge we find not merely a variety of interests, even of passionate interests; it is all one passion expressed through them all: poetry was for them the expression of a totality of unified interests.

I have tried to exhibit the criticism of Dryden and of Johnson, in this very brief review, in its appropriateness to their periods of history, periods when there was, for the purpose of literary determination, a *stasis*. And to exhibit that of Wordsworth and Coleridge as the criticism of an age of change. Even if it be true that change is always making ready, underneath, during a stable period, and that a period of change contains within itself the elements of limitation which will bring it to a halt, yet some stabilisations are more deeply founded than others. It is with Matthew Arnold that we come to a period of apparent stabilisation which was shallow and premature.

NOTE ON MR. HERBERT READ'S APPRAISAL
OF THE POETRY OF WORDSWORTH

There is a view of English poetry, already of some antiquity, which considers the main line of English poetry from Milton to Wordsworth, or from perhaps even before Milton, as an unfortunate interlude during which the English muse was, if not beside herself, at least not in possession of her faculties. I am sorry to find this view, which was largely Wordsworth's own, re-stated and confirmed by Mr. Herbert Read. Mr. Read is one of a few contemporaries, like Mr. Richards, with whom I almost never feel quite happy in disagreeing; but when, in his admirable small essay, *Form in Modern Poetry*, he writes as follows, I can only exclaim, "What are we coming to?":

> The main tradition of English poetry . . . begins with Chaucer and reaches its final culmination in Shakespeare. It is contradicted by most French poetry before Baudelaire, by the so-called classical phase of English poetry culminating in Alexander Pope, and by the late Poet Laureate. It was re-established in England by Wordsworth and Coleridge, developed in some degree by Browning and Gerard Manley Hopkins, and in our own day by poets like Wilfred Owen, Ezra Pound and T. S. Eliot.

To some extent I am in agreement; that is, I dare say that my valuation of the earlier poets, poet for poet, would approximate closely enough to Mr. Read's; and my admiration for the late Poet Laureate is as moderate as his, though I suspect a slight wilfulness in bringing him into this context. But I observe first that Mr. Read goes Wordsworth one better and excludes Milton; and when a poet has done as big a job as Milton, is it helpful to suggest that he has just been up a blind alley? And is Blake too minor a poet to count? As for French poetry, Mr. Read saves the situation with the qualification "most," so that I suppose Baudelaire's master Racine just squeaks in. And is it not arbitrary to assert that the "classical phase" of English poetry (if we are to employ that term at all) culminates in Pope? Surely Johnson belongs to it, and, with a touch of sentimentalism and even mawkishness, Gray and Collins; and where would Landor be but for the classical tradition? I hasten to add Mr. Read's next remark: "The distinction is not merely that between 'classical' and 'romantic.' This division cuts across in a different direction." I think that I understand this qualification, and if I understand I agree; nevertheless Mr. Read seems to have been using the term "classical" in two different meanings. Mr. Read's divisions are too clear-cut to leave my mind at ease. He considers that the poetic process of a mind like Dryden's and that of a mind like Wordsworth's are essentially diverse; and he says roundly of Dryden's art, "Such art is not poetry." Now I cannot see why Dryden's and Wordsworth's minds should have worked any more differently from each other than those of any other two poets. I do not believe that any two poets' minds work quite in the same way, so far as we can know enough about the matter for "working" to mean anything at all; I do not believe that even the same poet's mind need work in the same way in two different but equally good poems; but there must also be something in common in the poetic process of all poets' minds. Mr. Read quotes, in support of his contention, a passage from the *Annus Mirabilis* which I have not given:

> The Composition of all poems is or ought to be of wit; and wit in the Poet, or *wit writing* (if you will give me leave to use a School distinction), is no other than the faculty of imagination in the Writer; which, like a nimble Spaniel, beats over and ranges through the field of Memory, till it springs the Quarry it hunted after; or, without metaphor, which searches over all the Memory for the Species or Ideas of those things which it designs to represent. *Wit written* is that which is well defined, the happy result of Thought, or product of Imagination.

I should have thought this merely a happy description, in the language available at Dryden's time, and at a less profound level of insight than that of Coleridge or Wordsworth at their best, of the same sort of process that the latter were attempting to describe in language nearer to our own. But Mr. Read says No, what Dryden is talking about is something different: it is *wit written*, not poetry. Mr. Read seems to me to have fallen into the error which I mentioned in the text, of thinking that Dryden is only talking of his own kind of poetic composition, and that he was quite incapable of appreciating Chaucer and Shakespeare. Yet all that I myself have to go upon, in the end, is the kind of enjoyment that I get from Dryden's poetry.

The difference of opinion might be put in a metaphor. In reviewing English poetry, Mr. Read seems to charge himself with the task of casting out devils — though less drastically than Mr. Pound, who leaves nothing but a room well swept and not garnished. What I see, in the history of English poetry, is not so much daemonic possession as the splitting up of personality. If we say that one of these partial personalities which may develop in a national mind is that which manifested itself in the period between Dryden and Johnson, then what we have to do is to re-integrate it: otherwise we are likely to get only successive alternations of personality. Surely the great poet is, among other things, one who not merely restores a tradition which has been in abeyance, but one who in his poetry re-twines as many straying strands of tradition as possible. Nor can you isolate poetry from everything else in the history of a people; and it is rather strong to suggest that the English mind has been deranged ever since the time of Shakespeare, and that only recently have a few fitful rays of reason penetrated its darkness. If the malady is as chronic as that, it is pretty well beyond cure.

SHELLEY AND KEATS

February 17th, 1933

IT WOULD appear that the revolution effected by
Wordsworth was very far-reaching indeed. He
was not the first poet to present himself as the inspired
prophet, nor indeed is this quite Wordsworth's case.
Blake may have pretended, and with some claim, to
have penetrated mysteries of heaven and hell, but no
claim that Blake might make seems to descend upon
the "poet" in general; Blake simply had the visions,
and made use of poetry to set them forth. Scott, and
Byron in his more popular works, were merely society
entertainers. Wordsworth is really the first, in the
unsettled state of affairs in his time, to annex new authority for the poet, to meddle with social affairs, and
to offer a new kind of religious sentiment which it
seemed the peculiar prerogative of the poet to inter-
pret. Since Matthew Arnold made his Selections from
Wordsworth's poetry, it has become a commonplace
to observe that Wordsworth's true greatness as poet
is independent of his opinions, of his theory of diction
or of his nature-philosophy, and that it is found in
poems in which he has no ulterior motive whatever.
I am not sure that this critical eclecticism cannot go
too far; that we can judge and enjoy a man's poetry
while leaving wholly out of account all of the things
for which he cared deeply, and on behalf of which he
turned his poetry to account. If we dismiss Wordsworth's interests and beliefs, just how much, I wonder,

remains? To retain them, or to keep them in mind instead of deliberately extruding them in preparation for enjoying his poetry, is that not necessary to appreciate how great a poet Wordsworth really is? Consider, for instance, one of the very finest poets of the first part of the nineteenth century: Landor. He is an undoubted master of verse and prose; he is the author of at least one long poem which deserves to be much more read than it is; but his reputation has never been such as to bring him into comparison with Wordsworth or with either of the younger poets with whom we have now to deal. It is not only by reason of a handful of poems or a number of isolated lines expressive of deeper emotion than that of which Landor was capable, that we give Wordsworth his place; there is something integral about such greatness, and something significant in his place in the pattern of history, with which we have to reckon. And in estimating for ourselves the greatness of a poet we have to take into account also the *history* of his greatness. Wordsworth is an essential part of history; Landor only a magnificent by-product.

Shelley both had views about poetry and made use of poetry for expressing views. With Shelley we are struck from the beginning by the number of things poetry is expected to do; from a poet who tells us, in a note on vegetarianism, that "the orang-outang perfectly resembles man both in the order and the number of his teeth," we shall not know what not to expect. The notes to *Queen Mab* express, it is true, only the views of an intelligent and enthusiastic schoolboy, but a schoolboy who knows how to write; and throughout his work, which is of no small bulk for a short life, he does not, I think, let us forget that he took his ideas seriously. The ideas of Shelley seem to me always to be ideas of adolescence — as there is every reason why they should be. And an enthusiasm for Shelley seems to me also to be an affair of adolescence: for most of us, Shelley has marked an intense period before maturity, but for how many does Shelley remain the companion of age? I confess that I never open the volume of his poems simply because I want to read poetry, but only with some special reason for reference. I find his ideas repellant; and the difficulty of separating Shelley from his ideas and beliefs is still greater than with Wordsworth. And the biographical interest which Shelley has always excited makes it difficult to read the poetry without remembering the man: and the man was humourless, pedantic, self-centred, and sometimes almost a blackguard. Except for an occasional flash of shrewd sense, when he is speaking of someone else and not concerned with his own affairs or with fine writing, his letters are insufferably dull. He makes an astonishing contrast with the attractive Keats. On the other hand, I admit that Wordsworth does not present a very pleasing personality either; yet I not only enjoy his poetry as I cannot enjoy Shelley's, but I enjoy it more than when I first read it. I can only try to fumble (abating my prejudices as best I can) for reasons why Shelley's abuse of poetry does me more violence than Wordsworth's.

Shelley seems to have had to a high degree the un-usual faculty of passionate apprehension of abstract ideas. Whether he was not sometimes confused about his own feelings, as we may be tempted to believe when confounded by the philosophy of *Epipsychidion*, is another matter. I do not mean that Shelley had a metaphysical or philosophical mind; his mind was in some ways a very confused one: he was able to be at once and with the same enthusiasm an eighteenth-century rationalist and a cloudy Platonist. But ab-stractions could excite in him strong emotion. His views remained pretty fixed, though his poetic gift matured. It is open to us to guess whether his mind would have matured too; certainly, in his last, and to my mind greatest though unfinished poem, *The Tri-umph of Life*, there is evidence not only of better writ-ing than in any previous long poem, but of greater wisdom:

> Then what I thought was an old root that grew
> To strange distortion out of the hillside,
> Was indeed one of those (*sic*) deluded crew
> And that the grass, which methought hung so wide
> And white, was but his thin discoloured hair
> And that the holes he vainly sought to hide
> Were or had been eyes . . .

There is a precision of image and an economy here that is new to Shelley. But so far as we can judge, he never quite escaped from the tutelage of Godwin, even when he saw through the humbug as a man; and the weight of Mrs. Shelley must have been pretty heavy too. And, taking his work as it is, and without vain conjectures about the future, we may ask: is it possible to ignore the "ideas" in Shelley's poems, so as to be able to enjoy the poetry?

Mr. I. A. Richards deserves the credit of having done the pioneer work in the problem of Belief in the enjoyment of poetry; and any methodical pursuit of the problem I must leave to him and to those who are qualified after him. But Shelley raises the question in another form than that in which it presented itself to me in a note on the subject which I appended to an essay on Dante. There, I was concerned with two hypothetical readers, one of whom accepts the philosophy of the poet, and the other of whom rejects it; and so long as the poets in question were such as Dante and Lucretius, this seemed to cover the matter. I am not a Buddhist, but some of the early Buddhist scriptures affect me as parts of the Old Testament do; I can still enjoy Fitzgerald's *Omar*, though I do not hold that rather smart and shallow view of life. But some of Shelley's views I positively dislike, and that hampers my enjoyment of the poems in which they occur; and others seem to me so puerile that I cannot enjoy the poems in which they occur. And I do not find it possible to skip these passages and satisfy myself with the poetry in which no proposition pushes itself forward to claim assent. What complicates the problem still further is that in poetry so fluent as Shelley's there is a good deal which is just bad jingling. The following, for instance:

> On a battle-trumpet's blast
> I fled hither, fast, fast, fast,
> Mid the darkness upward cast.

> From the dust of creeds outworn,
> From the tyrant's banner torn,
> Gathering round me, onward borne,
> There was mingled many a cry —
> Freedom! Hope! Death! Victory!

Walter Scott seldom fell as low as this, though Byron more often. But in such lines, harsh and untunable, one is all the more affronted by the ideas, the ideas which Shelley bolted whole and never assimilated, visible in the catchwords of creeds outworn, tyrants and priests, which Shelley employed with such re-iteration. And the bad parts of a poem can contaminate the whole, so that when Shelley rises to the heights, at the end of the poem:

> To suffer woes which Hope thinks infinite;
> To forgive wrongs darker than death or night;
> To defy Power, which seems omnipotent;
> To love, and bear; to hope till Hope creates
> From its own wreck the thing it contemplates . . .

lines to the content of which belief is neither given nor denied, we are unable to enjoy them fully. One does not expect a poem to be equally sustained throughout; and in some of the most successful long poems there is a relation of the more tense to the more relaxed passages which is itself part of the pattern of beauty. But good lines amongst bad can never give more than a regretful pleasure. In reading *Epipsychidion* I am thoroughly gravelled by lines like:

> True love in this differs from dross or clay,
> That to divide is not to take away . . .
> I never was attached to that great sect
> Whose doctrine is, that each one should select

> Out of the crowd, a mistress or a friend
> And all the rest, though fair and wise, commend
> To cold oblivion . . .

so that when I come, a few lines later, upon a lovely image like:

> A vision like incarnate April, warning
> With smiles and tears, Frost the anatomy
> Into his summer grave,

I am as much shocked at finding it in such indifferent company as pleased by finding it at all. And we must admit that Shelley's finest long poems, as well as some of his worst, are those in which he took his ideas very seriously.[1] It was these ideas that blew the "fading coal" to life; no more than with Wordsworth can we ignore them without getting something no more Shelley's poetry than a wax effigy would be Shelley.

Shelley said that he disliked didactic poetry; but his own poetry is chiefly didactic, though (in fairness) not exactly in the sense in which he was using that word. Shelley's professed view of poetry is not dissimilar to that of Wordsworth. The language in which he clothes it in the "Defence of Poetry" is very magniloquent, and with the exception of the magnificent image which Joyce quotes somewhere in *Ulysses* ("the mind in creation is as a fading coal, which some invisible influence, like an inconstant wind, awakens to transitory brightness") it seems to me an inferior piece of writing to Wordsworth's great

---

[1] He did not, for instance, appear to take his ideas very seriously in *The Witch of Atlas*, which, with all its charm, I think we may dismiss as a trifle.

preface. He says other fine things too; but the following is more significant of the way in which he relates poetry to the social activity of the age:

The most unfailing herald, companion and follower of the awakening of a great people to work a beneficial change in opinion or institution, is poetry. At such periods there is an accumulation of the power of communicating and receiving intense and impassioned conceptions respecting man and nature. The persons in whom this power resides may often, so far as regards many portions of their nature, have little apparent correspondence with that spirit of good of which they are the ministers. But even whilst they deny and abjure, they are yet compelled to serve, the power which is seated on the throne of their own soul.

I know not whether Shelley had in mind, in his reservations about "the persons in whom this power resides," the defects of Byron or those of Wordsworth; he is hardly likely to have been contemplating his own. But this is a statement, and is either true or false. If he is suggesting that great poetry always tends to accompany a popular "change in opinion or institution," that we know to be false. Whether at such periods the power of "communicating and receiving intense and impassioned conceptions respecting man and nature" accumulates is doubtful; one would expect people to be too busy in other ways. Shelley does not appear, in this passage, to imply that poetry itself helps to operate these changes, and accumulate this power, nor does he assert that poetry is a usual by-product of change of these kinds; but he does affirm some relation between the two; and in consequence, a particular relation between his own poetry and the events of his own time; from which it would follow that the two throw light upon each other. This is perhaps the first appearance of the kinetic or revolutionary theory of poetry; for Wordsworth did not generalise to this point.

We may now return to the question how far it is possible to enjoy Shelley's poetry without approving the use to which he put it; that is, without sharing his views and sympathies. Dante, of course, was about as thoroughgoing a didacticist as one could find; and I have maintained elsewhere, and still maintain, that it is not essential to share Dante's beliefs in order to enjoy his poetry.[1] If in this instance I may appear to be extending the tolerance of a biassed mind, the example of Lucretius will do as well: one may share the essential beliefs of Dante and yet enjoy Lucretius to the full. Why then should this general indemnity not extend to Wordsworth and to Shelley? Here Mr. Richards comes very patly to our help:[2]

Coleridge, when he remarked that a "willing suspension of disbelief" accompanied much poetry, was noting an important fact, but not quite in the happiest terms, for we are neither aware of a disbelief nor voluntarily suspending it in these cases. It is better to say that the question of belief or disbelief, in the intellectual sense, never arises when we are reading well. If unfortunately it does arise, either through the poet's fault or our own, we have for the mo-

[1] Mr. A. E. Housman has affirmed (*The Name and Nature of Poetry*, p. 34) that "good religious poetry, whether in Keble or Dante or Job, is likely to be most justly appreciated and most discriminatingly relished by the undevout." There is a hard atom of truth in this, but if taken literally it would end in nonsense.

[2] *Practical Criticism*, p. 277.

ment ceased to be reading and have become astronomers, or theologians, or moralists, persons engaged in quite a different type of activity.

We may be permitted to infer, in so far as the distaste of a person like myself for Shelley's poetry is not attributable to irrelevant prejudices or to a simple blind spot, but is due to a peculiarity in the poetry and not in the reader, that it is not the presentation of beliefs which I do not hold, or — to put the case as extremely as possible — of beliefs that excite my abhorrence, that makes the difficulty. Still less is it that Shelley is deliberately making use of his poetic gifts to propagate a doctrine; for Dante and Lucretius did the same thing. I suggest that the position is somewhat as follows. When the doctrine, theory, belief, or "view of life" presented in a poem is one which the mind of the reader can accept as coherent, mature, and founded on the facts of experience, it interposes no obstacle to the reader's enjoyment, whether it be one that he accept or deny, approve or deprecate. When it is one which the reader rejects as childish or feeble, it may, for a reader of well-developed mind, set up an almost complete check. I observe in passing that we may distinguish, but without precision, between poets who employ their verbal, rhythmic and imaginative gift in the service of ideas which they hold passionately, and poets who employ the ideas which they hold with more or less settled conviction as material for a poem; poets may vary indefinitely between these two hypothetical extremes, and at what point we place any particular poet must remain incapable of exact calculation. And I am inclined to think that the reason why I was intoxicated by Shelley's poetry at the age of fifteen, and now find it almost unreadable, is not so much that at that age I accepted his ideas, and have since come to reject them, as that at that age "the question of belief or disbelief," as Mr. Richards puts it, did not arise. It is not so much that thirty years ago I was able to read Shelley under an illusion which experience has dissipated, as that because the question of belief or disbelief did not arise I was in a much better position to enjoy the poetry. I can only regret that Shelley did not live to put his poetic gifts, which were certainly of the first order, at the service of more tenable beliefs — which need not have been, for my purposes, beliefs more acceptable to me.

There is, however, more to the problem than that. I was struck by a sentence in Mr. Aldous Huxley's Introduction to D. H. Lawrence's Letters. "How bitterly," he says of Lawrence, "he loathed the Wilhelm-Meisterish view of love as an education, as a means to culture, a Sandow-exerciser for the soul!" Precisely; Lawrence in my opinion was right; but that view runs through the work of Goethe, and if you dislike it, what are you going to do about Goethe? Does "culture" require that we make (what Lawrence never did, and I respect him for it) a deliberate effort to put out of mind all our convictions and passionate beliefs about life when we sit down to read poetry? If so, so much the worse for culture. Nor, on the other hand, may we distinguish, as people sometimes do, between the occasions on which a particular poet is "being a poet" and the occasions on which he is "being a preacher." That is too facile. If you attempt to edit Shelley, or Wordsworth or Goethe in this way, there is no one point at which you must stop rather than another, and what you get in the end by this process is something which is not Shelley, or Wordsworth or Goethe at all, but a mere unrelated heap of charming stanzas, the débris of poetry rather than the poetry itself. And by using, or abusing, this principle of isolation you are in danger of seeking from poetry some illusory *pure* enjoyment, of separating poetry from everything else in the world, and cheating yourself out of a great deal that poetry has to give to your development.

Some years ago I tried to make the point, in a paper on Shakespeare, that Dante possessed a "philosophy" in a sense in which Shakespeare held none, or none of any importance. I have reason to believe that I did not succeed in making the point clear at all. Surely, people say, Shakespeare held a "philosophy," even though it cannot be formulated; surely our reading of Shakespeare gives us a deeper and wider understanding of life and death. And although I was anxious not to give such an impression, I seem to have given some readers to think that I was thereby estimating the poetry of Shakespeare as of less value than Dante's. People tend to believe that there is just some one essence of poetry, for which we can find the formula, and that poets can be ranged according to their possession of a greater or less quantity of this essence. Dante and Lucretius expounded explicit philosophies, as

Shakespeare did not. This simple distinction is very clear, but not necessarily highly important. What is important is what distinguishes all of these poets from such poets as Wordsworth, Shelley and Goethe. And here again I think that Mr. Richards can throw some light on the matter.

I believe that for a poet to be also a philosopher he would have to be virtually two men; I cannot think of any example of this thorough schizophrenia, nor can I see anything to be gained by it: the work is better performed inside two skulls than one. Coleridge is the apparent example, but I believe that he was only able to exercise the one activity at the expense of the other. A poet may borrow a philosophy or he may do without one. It is when he philosophises upon his own *poetic* insight that he is apt to go wrong. A great deal of the weakness of modern poetry is accounted for in a few pages of Mr. Richards's short essay, *Science and Poetry*; and although he has there D. H. Lawrence under specific examination, a good deal of what he says applies to the Romantic generation as well. "To distinguish," he says, "an intuition of an emotion from an intuition *by* it is not always easy." I believe that Wordsworth was inclined to the same error of which Mr. Richards finds Lawrence guilty. The case of Shelley is rather different: he borrowed ideas — which, as I have said, is perfectly legitimate — but he borrowed shabby ones, and when he had got them he muddled them up with his own intuitions. Of Goethe perhaps it is truer to say that he dabbled in both philosophy and poetry and made no great success of either; his true rôle was that of the man of the world and sage — a La Rochefoucauld, a La Bruyère, a Vauvenargues.

On the other hand, I should consider it a false simplification to present any of these poets, or Lawrence of whom Mr. Richards was speaking, simply as a case of *individual error*, and leave it at that. It is not a wilful paradox to assert that the greatness of each of these writers is indissolubly attached to his practice of the error, of his own specific variation of the error. Their place in history, their importance for their own and subsequent generations, is involved in it; this is not a purely personal matter. They would not have been as great as they were but for the limitations which prevented them from being greater than they were. They belong with the numbers of the great heretics of all times. This gives them a significance quite other than that of Keats, a singular figure in a varied and remarkable period.

Keats seems to me also a great poet. I am not happy about *Hyperion*: it contains great lines, but I do not know whether it is a great poem. The Odes — especially perhaps the *Ode to Psyche* — are enough for his reputation. But I am not so much concerned with the degree of his greatness as with its kind; and its kind is manifested more clearly in his Letters than in his poems; and in contrast with the kinds we have been reviewing, it seems to me to be much more the kind of Shakespeare.[1] The Letters are certainly the

---

[1] I have not read Mr. Murry's *Keats and Shakespeare*: perhaps I say no more than Mr. Murry has said better and more exhaustively in that

most notable and the most important ever written by any English poet. Keats's egotism, such as it is, is that of youth which time would have redeemed. His letters are what letters ought to be; the fine things come in unexpectedly, neither introduced nor shown out, but between trifle and trifle. His observations suggested by Wordsworth's *Gypsey*, in a letter to Bailey of 1817, are of the finest quality of criticism, and the deepest penetration:

It seems to me that if Wordsworth had thought a little deeper at that moment, he would not have written the poem at all. I should judge it to have been written in one of the most comfortable moods of his life — it is a kind of sketchy intellectual landscape, not a search for truth.

And in a letter to the same correspondent a few days later he says:

In passing, however, I must say one thing that has pressed upon me lately, and increased my Humility and capability of submission — and that is this truth — Men of Genius are great as certain ethereal chemicals operating on the Mass of neutral intellect — but they have not any individuality, any determined character — I would call the top and head of those who have a proper self Men of Power.[1]

This is the sort of remark, which, when made by a man so young as was Keats, can only be called the

book; I am sure that he has meditated the matter much more deeply than I have.

[1] Mr. Herbert Read quotes this passage in his *Form in Modern Poetry*, but pursues his speculations to a point to which I would not willingly follow him.

result of genius. There is hardly one statement of Keats about poetry, which, when considered carefully and with due allowance for the difficulties of communication, will not be found to be true; and what is more, true for greater and more mature poetry than anything that Keats ever wrote.

But I am being tempted into a descant upon the general brilliance and profundity of the observations scattered through Keats's letters, and should probably be tempted further into remarking upon their merit as models of correspondence (not that one should ever take a model in letter-writing) and their revelation of a charming personality. My design, in this very narrow frame, has been only to refer to them as evidence of a very different kind of poetic mind than any of those I have just been considering. Keats's sayings about poetry, thrown out in the course of private correspondence, keep pretty close to intuition; and they have no apparent bearing upon his own times, as he himself does not appear to have taken any absorbing interest in public affairs — though when he did turn to such matters, he brought to bear a shrewd and penetrating intellect. Wordsworth had a very delicate sensibility to social life and social changes. Wordsworth and Shelley both theorise. Keats has no theory, and to have formed one was irrelevant to his interests, and alien to his mind. If we take either Wordsworth or Shelley as representative of his age, as being a voice of the age, we cannot so take Keats. But we cannot accuse Keats of any withdrawal, or refusal; he was merely about his business. He had no theories, yet in the sense appropriate to the poet, in the same sense, though to a lesser degree than Shakespeare, he had a "philosophic" mind. He was occupied only with the highest use of poetry; but that does not imply that poets of other types may not rightly and sometimes by obligation be concerned about the other uses.

MATTHEW ARNOLD

March 3rd, 1933

THE rise of the democracy to power in America and Europe is not, as has been hoped, to be a safeguard of peace and civilisation. It is the rise of the uncivilised, whom no school education can suffice to provide with intelligence and reason. It looks as if the world were entering upon a new stage of experience, unlike anything heretofore, in which there must be a new discipline of suffering to fit men for the new conditions."

I have quoted the foregoing words, partly because they are by Norton [1] and partly because they are not by Arnold. The first two sentences might well be Arnold's. But the third — "a new stage of experience, unlike anything heretofore, in which there must be a new discipline of suffering": these words are not only not Arnold's, but we know at once that they could not have been written by him. Arnold hardly looks ahead to the new stage of experience; and though he speaks to us of discipline, it is the discipline of culture, not the discipline of suffering. Arnold represents a period of stasis; of relative and precarious stability, it is true, a brief halt in the endless march of humanity in some, or in any direction. Arnold is neither a reactionary nor a revolutionary; he marks a period of time, as do Dryden and Johnson before him.

[1] Letter to Leslie Stephen, January 8th, 1896.

Even if the delight we get from Arnold's writings, prose and verse, be moderate, yet he is in some respects the most satisfactory man of letters of his age. You remember the famous judgement which he pronounced upon the poets of the epoch which I have just been considering; a judgement which, at its time, must have appeared startlingly independent. "The English poetry of the first quarter of this century," he says in his essay on *The Function of Criticism*, "with plenty of energy, plenty of creative force, did not know enough." We should be right too, I think, if we added that Carlyle, Ruskin, Tennyson, Browning, with plenty of energy, plenty of creative force, had not enough wisdom. Their culture was not always well-rounded; their knowledge of the human soul was often partial and often shallow. Arnold was not a man of vast or exact scholarship, and he had neither walked in hell nor been rapt to heaven; but what he did know, of books and men, was in its way well-balanced and well-marshalled. After the prophetic frenzies of the end of the eighteenth and the beginning of the nineteenth century, he seems to come to us saying: "This poetry is very fine, it is opulent and careless, it is sometimes profound, it is highly original; but you will never establish and maintain a tradition if you go on in this haphazard way. There are minor virtues which have flourished better at other times and in other countries: these you must give heed to, these you must apply, in your poetry, in your prose, in your conversation and your way of living; else you condemn yourselves to enjoy only fitful and transient bursts of literary brilliance, and you will never, as a people, a nation, a race, have a fully formed tradition and personality." However well-nourished we may be on previous literature and previous culture, we cannot afford to neglect Arnold.

I have elsewhere tried to point out some of Arnold's weaknesses when he ventured into departments of thought for which his mind was unsuited and ill-equipped. In philosophy and theology he was an undergraduate; in religion a Philistine. It is a pleasanter task to define a man's limitations within the field in which he is qualified; for there, the definition of limitation may be at the same time a precision of the writer's excellences. Arnold's poetry has little technical interest. It is academic poetry in the best sense; the best fruit which can issue from the promise shown by the prize-poem. When he is not simply being himself, he is most at ease in a master's gown: *Empedocles on Etna* is one of the finest academic poems ever written. He tried other robes which became him less well; I cannot but think of *Tristram and Iseult* and *The Forsaken Merman* as charades. *Sohrab and Rustum* is a fine piece, but less fine than *Gebir*; and in the classical line Landor, with a finer ear, can beat Arnold every time. But Arnold is a poet to whom one readily returns. It is a pleasure, certainly, after associating with the riff-raff of the early part of the century, to be in the company of a man *qui sait se conduire*; but Arnold is something more than an agreeable Professor of Poetry. With all his fastidiousness and superciliousness and officiality, Arnold is more intimate with us than Browning, more intimate than Tennyson ever is except at moments, as in the passionate flights in *In Memoriam*. He is the poet and critic of a period of false stability. All his writing in the kind of *Literature and Dogma* seems to me a valiant attempt to dodge the issue, to mediate between Newman and Huxley; but his poetry, the best of it, is too honest to employ any but his genuine feelings of unrest, loneliness and dissatisfaction. Some of his limitations are manifest enough. In his essay on *The Study of Poetry* he has several paragraphs on Burns, and for an Englishman and an Englishman of his time, Arnold understands Burns very well. Perhaps I have a partiality for small oppressive nationalities like the Scots that makes Arnold's patronising manner irritate me; and certainly I suspect Arnold of helping to fix the wholly mistaken notion of Burns as a singular untutored English dialect poet, instead of as a decadent representative of a great alien tradition. But he says (taking occasion to rebuke the country in which Burns lived) that "no one can deny that it is of advantage to a poet to deal with a beautiful world"; and this remark strikes me as betraying a limitation. It is an advantage to mankind in general to live in a beautiful world; that no one can doubt. But for the poet is it so important? We mean all sorts of things, I know, by Beauty. But the essential advantage for a poet is not to have a beautiful world with which to deal: it is to be able to see beneath both beauty and ugliness; to see the boredom, and the horror, and the glory.

The vision of the horror and the glory was denied to

Arnold, but he knew something of the boredom. He speaks much of the "consolatory" power of Words-worth's poetry, and it is in connexion with Words-worth that he makes many of his wisest observations about poetry.

> But when will Europe's latter hour
> Again find Wordsworth's healing power?
> Others will teach us how to dare,
> And against fear our breast to steel:
> Others will strengthen us to bear —
> But who, ah who, will make us feel?
> The cloud of mortal destiny,
> Others will front it fearlessly —
> But who, like him, will put it by? [1]

His tone is always of regret, of loss of faith, instability, nostalgia:

> And love, if love, of happier men.
> Of happier men, for they, at least,
> Have *dreamed* two human hearts might blend
> In one, and were through faith released
> From isolation without end
> Prolonged, nor knew, although no less
> Alone than thou, their loneliness.

This is a familiar enough sentiment; and perhaps a more robust comment on the situation is, that if you don't like it, you can get on with it; and the verse itself is not highly distinguished. Marguerite, at best, is a shadowy figure, neither very passionately desired nor very closely observed, a mere pretext for lamen-

---

[1] I do not quote these lines as good verse. They are very carelessly written. The fourth line is particularly clumsy, the sixth has a bathetic repetition. To "put by" the cloud of human destiny is not a felicitous expression. The dashes at the end of two lines are a symptom of weakness, like Arnold's irritating use of italicised words.

tation. His personal emotion is indeed most convincing when he deals with an impersonal subject. And when we know his poetry, we are not surprised that in his criticism he tells us little or nothing about his experience of writing it, and that he is so little concerned with poetry from the maker's point of view. One feels that the writing of poetry brought him little of that excitement, that joyful loss of self in the workmanship of art, that intense and transitory relief which comes at the moment of completion and is the chief reward of creative work. As we can forget, in reading his criticism, that he is a poet himself, so it is all the more necessary to remind ourselves that his creative and his critical writing are essentially the work of the same man. The same weakness, the same necessity for something to depend upon, which make him an academic poet make him an academic critic.

From time to time, every hundred years or so, it is desirable that some critic shall appear to review the past of our literature, and set the poets and the poems in a new order. This task is not one of revolution but of readjustment. What we observe is partly the same scene, but in a different and more distant perspective; there are new and strange objects in the foreground, to be drawn accurately in proportion to the more familiar ones which now approach the horizon, where all but the most eminent become invisible to the naked eye. The exhaustive critic, armed with a powerful glass, will be able to sweep the distance and gain an acquaintance with minute objects in the landscape with which to compare minute objects close at hand; he will be able to gauge nicely the position and proportion of the objects surrounding us, in the whole of the vast panorama. This metaphorical fancy only represents the ideal; but Dryden, Johnson and Arnold have each performed the task as well as human frailty will allow. The majority of critics can be expected only to parrot the opinions of the last master of criticism; among more independent minds a period of destruction, of preposterous over-estimation, and of successive fashions takes place, until a new authority comes to introduce some order. And it is not merely the passage of time and accumulation of new artistic experience, nor the ineradicable tendency of the great majority of men to repeat the opinions of those few who have taken the trouble to think, nor the tendency of a nimble but myopic minority to progenerate heterodoxies, that makes new assessments necessary. It is that no generation is interested in Art in quite the same way as any other; each generation, like each individual, brings to the contemplation of art its own categories of appreciation, makes its own demands upon art, and has its own uses for art. "Pure" artistic appreciation is to my thinking only an ideal, when not merely a figment, and must be so long as the appreciation of art is an affair of limited and transient human beings existing in space and time. Both artist and audience are limited. There is for each time, for each artist, a kind of alloy required to make the metal workable into art; and each generation prefers its own alloy to any other. Hence each new master of criticism performs a useful service merely by the fact that his errors are of a different kind from the last; and the longer sequence of critics we have, the greater amount of correction is possible.

It was desirable after the surprising, varied and abundant contribution of the Romantic Period that this task of criticism should be undertaken again. Nothing that was done in this period was of the nature of what Arnold was able to do, because that was not the time in which it could be done. Coleridge, Lamb, Hazlitt, De Quincey, did work of great importance upon Shakespeare and the Elizabethan dramatists, and discovered new treasure which they left for others to calculate. The instruments of Arnold's time appear now, of course, very antiquated: his was the epoch of Ward's *English Poets*, and of *The Golden Treasury*, birthday albums and calendars with a poetical quotation for each day. Arnold was not Dryden or Johnson; he was an Inspector of Schools and he became Professor of Poetry. He was an educator. The valuation of the Romantic poets, in academic circles, is still very largely that which Arnold made. It was right, it was just, it was necessary for its time; and of course it had its defects. It is tinged by his own uncertainty, his own apprehensions, his own view of what it was best that his own time should believe; and it is very much influenced by his religious attitude. His taste is not comprehensive. He seems to have chosen, when he could—for much of his work is occasional—those subjects in connexion with which he could best express his views about morals and society: Wordsworth — perhaps not quite as Wordsworth would have recognised himself, Heine, Amiel, Guérin. He was capable of learning from France and from Germany. But the *use* to which he put poetry was limited; he wrote about poets when they provided a pretext for his sermon to the British public; and he was apt to think of the greatness of poetry rather than of its genuineness.

There is no poetry which Arnold experienced more deeply than that of Wordsworth; the lines which I quoted above are not so much a criticism of Wordsworth as a testimonial of what Wordsworth had done for *him*. We may expect to find in the essay on Wordsworth, if anywhere, a statement of what poetry meant to Arnold. It is in his essay on Wordsworth that occurs his famous definition: "Poetry is at bottom a criticism of life." At bottom: that is a great way down; the bottom is the bottom. At the bottom of the abyss is what few ever see, and what those cannot bear to look at for long; and it is not a "criticism of life." If we mean life as a whole — not that Arnold ever saw life as a whole — from top to bottom, can anything that we can say of it ultimately, of that awful mystery, be called criticism? We bring back very little from our rare descents, and that is not criticism. Arnold might just as well have said that Christian worship is at bottom a criticism of the Trinity. We see better what Arnold's words amount to when we recognise that his own poetry is decidedly critical poetry. A poem like *Heine's Grave* is criticism, and very fine criticism too; and a kind of criticism which is justified because it could not be made in prose. Sometimes Arnold's criticism is on a lower level:

> One morn, as through Hyde Park we walked,
> My friend and I, by chance we talked,
> Of Lessing's famed Laocoon.[1]

The poem about Heine is good poetry for the same reason that it is good criticism: because Heine is one of the *personae*, the masks, behind which Arnold is able to go through his performance. The reason why some criticism is good (I do not care to generalise here about all criticism) is that the critic assumes, in a way, the personality of the author whom he criticises, and through this personality is able to speak with his own voice. Arnold's Wordsworth is as much like Arnold as he is like Wordsworth. Sometimes a critic may choose an author to criticise, a rôle to assume, as far as possible the antithesis to himself, a personality which has actualised all that has been suppressed in himself; we can sometimes arrive at a very satisfactory intimacy with our anti-masks.

"The greatness of a poet," Arnold goes on to say, "lies in his powerful and beautiful application of ideas to life." Not a happy way of putting it, as if ideas were a lotion for the inflamed skin of suffering humanity. But it seems to be what Arnold thought he was doing. He presently qualifies this assertion by point-

---

[1] It may be said of Arnold's inferior work, as was said of that of an inferior poet, that he faggotted his verses as they fell. And if they rhymed and rattled, all was well. Of course we do not judge Arnold as a poet by such effusions as this, but we cannot be blamed for forming a lower opinion of his capacity for self-criticism. He need not have printed them.

ing out that "morals" must not be interpreted too narrowly:

> Morals are often treated in a narrow and false fashion; they are bound up with systems of thought and belief which have had their day; they are fallen into the hands of pedants and professional dealers; they grow tiresome to some of us.

Alas! for morals as Arnold conceived them; they are grown still more tiresome. He then remarks significantly in speaking of the "Wordsworthians":

> The Wordsworthians are apt to praise him for the wrong things, and to lay far too much stress upon what they call his philosophy. His poetry is the reality, his philosophy — so far, at least, as it may put on the form and habit of a "scientific system of thought," and the more that it puts them on — is the illusion. Perhaps we shall one day learn to make this proposition general, and to say: Poetry is the reality, philosophy the illusion.

This seems to me a striking, dangerous and subversive assertion. Poetry is at bottom a criticism of life; yet philosophy is illusion; the reality is the criticism of life. Arnold might have read Lessing's famed Laocoon with a view to disentangling his own confusions.

We must remember that for Arnold, as for everyone else, "poetry" meant a particular selection and order of poets. It meant, as for everyone else, the poetry that he liked, that he re-read; when we come to the point of making a statement about poetry, it is the poetry that sticks in our minds that weights that statement. And at the same time we notice that Arnold has come to an opinion about poetry different

from that of any of his predecessors. For Wordsworth and for Shelley poetry was a vehicle for one
kind of philosophy or another, but the philosophy
was something believed in. For Arnold the best poetry supersedes both religion and philosophy. I have
tried to indicate the results of this conjuring trick
elsewhere.[1] The most generalised form of my own
view is simply this: that nothing in this world or the
next is a substitute for anything else; and if you find
that you must do without something, such as religious
faith or philosophic belief, then you must just do
without it. I can persuade myself, I find, that some
of the things that I can hope to get are better worth
having than some of the things I cannot get; or I may
hope to alter myself so as to want different things;
but I cannot persuade myself that it is the same desires that are satisfied, or that I have in effect the
same thing under a different name.

A French friend said of the late York Powell of
Oxford: "*il était aussi tranquille dans son manque de foi
que le mystique dans sa croyance.*" You could not say
that of Arnold; his charm and his interest are largely
due to the painful position that he occupied between
faith and disbelief. Like many people the vanishing
of whose religious faith has left behind only habits, he
placed an exaggerated emphasis upon morals. Such
people often confuse morals with their own good habits, the result of a sensible upbringing, prudence, and
the absence of any very powerful temptation; but I
do not speak of Arnold or of any particular person,

[1] "Arnold and Pater," in *Selected Essays.*

for only God knows. Morals for the saint are only a preliminary matter; for the poet a secondary matter. How Arnold finds morals in poetry is not clear. He tells us that:

A poetry of revolt against moral ideas is a poetry of revolt against *life*; a poetry of indifference towards moral ideas is a poetry of indifference towards *life*,

but the statement left in suspension, and without Arnold's illustrating it by examples of poetic revolt and poetic indifference, seems to have little value. A little later he tells us why Wordsworth is great:

Wordsworth's poetry is great because of the extraordinary power with which Wordsworth feels the joy offered to us in nature, the joy offered to us in the simple primary affections and duties; and because of the extraordinary power with which, in case after case, he shows us this joy, and renders it so as to make us share it.

It is not clear whether "the simple primary affections and duties" (whatever they are, and however distinguished from the secondary and the complex) is meant to be an expansion of "nature," or another joy superadded: I rather think the latter, and take "nature" to mean the Lake District. I am not, furthermore, sure of the meaning of the conjunction of two quite different reasons for Wordsworth's greatness: one being the power with which Wordsworth *feels* the joy of nature, the other the power by which he makes us *share* it. In any case, it is definitely a communication theory, as any theory of the poet as teacher, leader, or priest is bound to be. One way of testing it is to ask why other poets are great. Can we say that Shakespeare's poetry is great because of the extraordinary power with which Shakespeare feels estimable feelings, and because of the extraordinary power with which he makes us share them? I enjoy Shakespeare's poetry to the full extent of my capacity for enjoying poetry; but I have not the slightest approach to certainty that I share Shakespeare's feelings; nor am I very much concerned to know whether I do or not. In short, Arnold's account seems to me to err in putting the emphasis upon the poet's feelings, instead of upon the poetry. We can say that in poetry there is communication from writer to reader, but should not proceed from this to think of the poetry as being primarily the vehicle of communication. Communication may take place, but will explain nothing. Or Arnold's statement may be criticised in another way, by asking whether Wordsworth would be a less great poet, if he felt with extraordinary power the horror offered to us in nature, and the boredom and sense of restriction in the simple primary affections and duties? Arnold seems to think that because, as he says, Wordsworth "deals with more of *life*" than Burns, Keats and Heine, he is dealing with more of moral ideas. A poetry which is concerned with moral ideas, it would appear, is concerned with life; and a poetry concerned with life is concerned with moral ideas.

This is not the place for discussing the deplorable moral and religious effects of confusing poetry and morals in the attempt to find a substitute for religious faith. What concerns me here, is the disturbance of our literary values in consequence of it. One observes this in Arnold's criticism. It is easy to see that Dryden underrated Chaucer; not so easy to see that to rate Chaucer as highly as Dryden did (in a period in which critics were not lavish of superlatives) was a triumph of objectivity for its time, as was Dryden's consistent differentiation between Shakespeare and Beaumont and Fletcher. It is easy to see that Johnson underrated Donne and overrated Cowley; it is even possible to come to understand why. But neither Johnson nor Dryden had any axe to grind; and in their errors they are more consistent than Arnold. Take, for instance, Arnold's opinion of Chaucer, a poet who, although very different from Arnold, was not altogether deficient in high seriousness. First he contrasts Chaucer with Dante: we admit the inferiority, and are almost convinced that Chaucer is not serious enough. But is Chaucer, in the end, less serious than Wordsworth, with whom Arnold does not compare him? And when Arnold puts Chaucer below François Villon, although he is in a way right, and although it was high time that somebody in England spoke up for Villon, one does not feel that the theory of "high seriousness" is in operation. That is one of the troubles of the critic who feels called upon to set the poets in rank: if he is honest with his own sensibility he must now and again violate his own rules of rating. There are also dangers arising from being too sure that one knows what "genuine poetry" is. Here is one very positive pronouncement:

The difference between genuine poetry and the poetry of Dryden, Pope and all their school, is briefly this: their poetry is conceived and composed in their wits, genuine poetry is conceived and composed in the soul. The difference between the two kinds of poetry is immense.[1]

And what, we wonder, had Arnold —

> For rigorous teachers seized his youth
> And purged its faith, and trimmed its fire,
> Showed him the high white star of Truth,
> There bade him gaze, and there aspire;
> > Even now their whispers pierce the gloom:
> > What dost thou in this living tomb?

what had a man whose youth was so rigorously seized and purged at Rugby, to do with an abstract entity like the Soul? "The difference between the two kinds of poetry is immense." But there are not two kinds of poetry, but many kinds; and the difference here is no more immense than that between the kind of Shakespeare and the kind of Arnold. There is petulance in such a judgement, arrogance and excess of heat. It was justifiable for Coleridge and Wordsworth and Keats to depreciate Dryden and Pope, in the ardour of the changes which they were busy about; but Arnold was engaged in no revolution, and his short-sightedness can only be excused.

I do not mean to suggest that Arnold's conception

---

[1] Practically the same distinction as that of Arnold is maintained, though with more subtlety and persuasiveness, by Mr. Housman in his *Name and Nature of Poetry*. A newer and more radical classification to the same effect is that of Mr. Herbert Read already quoted.

of the use of poetry, an educator's view, vitiates his criticism. To ask of poetry that it give religious and philosophic satisfaction, while deprecating philosophy and dogmatic religion, is of course to embrace the shadow of a shade. But Arnold had real taste. His preoccupations, as I have said, make him too exclusively concerned with *great* poetry, and with the greatness of it. His view of Milton is for this reason unsatisfying. But you cannot read his essay on *The Study of Poetry* without being convinced by the felicity of his quotations: to be able to quote as Arnold could is the best evidence of taste. The essay is a classic in English criticism: so much is said in so little space, with such economy and with such authority. Yet he was so conscious of what, for him, poetry was *for*, that he could not altogether see it for what it is. And I am not sure that he was highly sensitive to the musical qualities of verse. His own occasional bad lapses arouse the suspicion; and so far as I can recollect he never emphasises this virtue of poetic style, this fundamental, in his criticism. What I call the "auditory imagination" is the feeling for syllable and rhythm, penetrating far below the conscious levels of thought and feeling, invigorating every word; sinking to the most primitive and forgotten, returning to the origin and bringing something back, seeking the beginning and the end. It works through meanings, certainly, or not without meanings in the ordinary sense, and fuses the old and obliterated and the trite, the current, and the new and surprising, the most ancient and the most civilised mentality. Arnold's notion of "life," in his account of poetry, does not perhaps go deep enough.

I feel, rather than observe, an inner uncertainty and lack of confidence and conviction in Matthew Arnold: the conservatism which springs from lack of faith, and the zeal for reform which springs from dislike of change. Perhaps, looking inward and finding how little he had to support him, looking outward on the state of society and its tendencies, he was somewhat disturbed. He had no real serenity, only an impeccable demeanour. Perhaps he cared too much for civilisation, forgetting that Heaven and Earth shall pass away, and Mr. Arnold with them, and there is only one stay. He is a representative figure. A man's theory of the place of poetry is not independent of his view of life in general.

THE MODERN MIND

March 17th, 1933

THERE is a sentence in Maritain's *Art and Scho-lasticism* which occurs to me in this context: "Work such as Picasso's," he says, "shows a fearful progress in self-consciousness on the part of painting."

So far I have drawn a few light sketches to indicate the changes in the self-consciousness of poets thinking about poetry. A thorough history of this "progress in self-consciousness" in poetry and the criticism of poetry would have kinds of criticism to consider which do not fall within the narrow scope of these lectures: the history of Shakespeare criticism alone, in which, for instance, Morgann's Essay on the character of Falstaff and Coleridge's *Lectures on Shakespeare* would be representative moments, would have to be considered in some detail. But we have observed the notable development in self-consciousness in Dryden's Prefaces, and in the first serious attempt, which he made, at a valuation of the English poets. We have seen his work in one direction continued, and a method perfected, by Johnson in his careful estimation of a number of poets, an estimate arrived at by the application of what are on the whole admirably consistent standards. We have found a deeper insight into the nature of the poetic activity in remarks scattered through the writings of Coleridge and in the Preface of Wordsworth and in the Letters of Keats; and a perception, still immature, of the need

to elucidate the social function of poetry in Wordsworth's *Preface* and in Shelley's *Defence*. In the criticism of Arnold we find a continuation of the work of
the Romantic poets with a new appraisal of the poetry
of the past by a method which, lacking the precision
of Johnson's, gropes towards wider and deeper con-
nexions. I have not wished to exhibit this "progress
in self-consciousness" as being necessarily *progress*
with an association of higher value. For one thing, it
cannot be wholly abstracted from the general changes
in the human mind in history; and that these changes
have any teleological significance is not one of my
assumptions.

Arnold's insistence upon order in poetry according
to a moral valuation was, for better or worse, of the
first importance for his age. When he is not at his
best he obviously falls between two stools. Just as his
poetry is too reflective, too ruminative, to rise ever
to the first rank, so also is his criticism. He is not, on
the one hand, quite a pure enough poet to have the
sudden illuminations which we find in the criticism of
Wordsworth, Coleridge and Keats; and on the other
hand he lacked the mental discipline, the passion for
exactness in the use of words and for consistency and
continuity of reasoning, which distinguishes the philosopher. He sometimes confuses words and meanings: neither as poet nor as philosopher should he
have been satisfied with such an utterance as that
"poetry is at bottom a criticism of life." A more profound insight into poetry and a more exact use of
language than Arnold's are required. The critical

method of Arnold, the assumptions of Arnold, remained valid for the rest of his century. In quite
diverse developments, it is the criticism of Arnold
that sets the tone: Walter Pater, Arthur Symons,
Addington Symonds, Leslie Stephen, F. W. H. Myers,
George Saintsbury — all the more eminent critical
names of the time bear witness to it.

Whether we agree or not with any or all of his conclusions, whether we admit or deny that his method
is adequate, we must admit that the work of Mr. I. A.
Richards will have been of cardinal importance in the
history of his literary criticism. Even if his criticism
proves to be entirely on the wrong track, even if this
modern "self-consciousness" turns out to be only a
blind alley, Mr. Richards will have done something in
accelerating the exhaustion of the possibilities. He will
have helped indirectly to discredit the criticism of
persons qualified neither by sensibility nor by knowledge of poetry, from which we suffer daily. There is
some hope of greater clarity; we should begin to learn
to distinguish the appreciation of poetry from theorising about poetry, and to know when we are not talking about poetry but about something else suggested
by it. There are two elements in Richards's scheme,
both of considerable importance for its ultimate
standing, of which I have the gravest doubts but
with which I am not here concerned: his theory of
Value and his theory of Education (or rather the
theory of Education assumed in or implied by his
attitude in *Practical Criticism*). As for psychology
and linguistics, that is his field and not mine. I am

more concerned here with what seem to me to be a few unexamined assumptions that he has made. I do not know whether he still adheres to certain assertions made in his early essay *Science and Poetry*; but I do not understand that he has yet made any public modification of them. Here is one that is in my mind:

> The most dangerous of the sciences is only now beginning to come into action. I am thinking less of Psychoanalysis or of Behaviourism than of the whole subject which includes them. It is very probable that the Hindenburg Line to which the defence of our traditions retired as a result of the onslaughts of the last century will be blown up in the near future. If this should happen a mental chaos such as man has never experienced may be expected. We shall then be thrown back, as Matthew Arnold foresaw, upon poetry. Poetry is capable of saving us. . . .

I should have felt completely at a loss in this passage, had not Matthew Arnold turned up; and then it seemed to me that I knew a little better what was what. I should say that an affirmation like this was highly characteristic of one type of modern mind. For one of the things that one can say about the modern mind is that it comprehends every extreme and degree of opinion. Here, from the essay, *Art and Scholasticism*, which I have already quoted, is Mr. Maritain:

> It is a deadly error to expect poetry to provide the super-substantial nourishment of man.

Mr. Maritain is a theologian as well as philosopher, and you may be sure that when he says "deadly error" he is in deadly earnest. But if the author of *Anti-Moderne* is hardly to be considered a "modern" man, we can find other varieties of opinion. In a book called *The Human Parrot*, Mr. Montgomery Belgion has two essays, one called *Art and Mr. Maritain* and the other *What is Criticism*, from which you will learn that neither Maritain nor Richards knows what he is talking about. Mr. Richards further maintains that the experience of poetry is not a mystical revelation, and the Abbé Henri Brémond,[1] in *Prayer and Poetry*, is concerned with telling us in what kind and degree it is. On this point Mr. Belgion is apparently in accord with Mr. Richards. And we may be wise to keep in mind a remark of Mr. Herbert Read in *Form in Modern Poetry*: "If a literary critic happens to be also a poet . . . he is liable to suffer from dilemmas which do not trouble the philosophic calm of his more prosaic colleagues."

Beyond a belief that poetry does something of importance, or has something of importance to do, there does not seem to be much agreement. It is interesting that in our time, which has not produced any vast number of important poets, so many people — and there are many more — should be asking questions about poetry. These problems are not those which properly concern poets as poets at all; if poets plunge into the discussion, it is probably because they have interests and curiosities outside of writing poetry. We need not summon those who call themselves Humanists (for they have for the most part not

[1] While preparing this book for press I learn with great regret of the Abbé Brémond's untimely death. It is a great pity that he could not have lived to complete the *Histoire du sentiment religieux en France.*

been primarily occupied with the nature and function of poetry) to bear witness that we have here the problem of religious faith and its substitutes. Not all contemporary critics, of course, but at least a number who appear to have little else in common, seem to consider that art, specifically poetry, has something to do with religion, though they disagree as to what this something may be. The relationship is not always envisaged so moralistically as it was by Arnold, nor so generally as in the statement by Mr. Richards which I quoted. For Mr. Belgion, for instance,

An outstanding example of poetic allegory is in the final canto of the *Paradiso*, where the poet seeks to give an allegorical account of the Beatific Vision, and then declares his efforts vain. We may read this over and over again, and in the end we shall no more have had a revelation of the nature of the Vision than we had before ever we had heard of either it or Dante.

Mr. Belgion seems to have taken Dante at his word. But what we experience as readers is never exactly what the poet experienced, nor would there be any point in its being, though certainly it has some relation to the poet's experience. What the poet experienced is not poetry but poetic material; the writing of the poetry is a fresh "experience" for him, and the reading of it, by the author or by anyone else, is another thing still. Mr. Belgion, in denying a theory which he attributes to Mr. Maritain, seems to me to make his own mistakes; but it is a religion-analogy which is in question. Mr. Richards is much occupied with the religious problem simply in the attempt to avoid it. In an appendix to the second edition of *Principles of Literary Criticism* he has a note on my own verse, which, being as favourable as I could desire, seems to me very acute. But he observes that Canto XXVI of the *Purgatorio* illuminates my "persistent concern with sex, the problem of our generation, as religion was the problem of the last." I readily admit the importance of Canto XXVI, and it was shrewd of Mr. Richards to notice it; but in his contrast of sex and religion he makes a distinction which is too subtle for me to grasp. One might think that sex and religion were "problems" like Free Trade and Imperial Preference; it seems odd that the human race should have gone on for so many thousands of years before it suddenly realised that religion and sex, one right after the other, presented problems.

It has been my view throughout — and it is only a commonplace after all — that the development and change of poetry and of the criticism of it is due to elements which enter from outside. I tried to draw attention not so much to the importance of Dryden's "contribution" to literary criticism, as if he were merely adding to a store of quantity, as to the importance of the fact that he should *want* to articulate and expound his views on drama and translation and on the English poetry of the past; and, when we came to Johnson, to call attention to the further development of an historical consciousness which made Johnson *want* to estimate, in more detail, the English poets of his own age and of previous ages;[1] and it seemed to me that Wordsworth's theories about poetry drew their aliment from social sources. To Matthew Arnold we owe the credit of bringing the religious issue explicitly into the discussion of literature and poetry; and with due respect to Mr. Richards, and with Mr. Richards himself as a witness, it does not seem to me that this "issue" has been wholly put aside and replaced by that of "sex." My contemporaries seem to me still to be occupied with it, whether they call themselves churchmen, or agnostics, or rationalists, or social revolutionists. The contrast between the doubts that our contemporaries express, and the questions that they ask and the problems they put themselves, and the attitude of at least a part of the past, was well put by Jacques Rivière in two sentences:

If in the seventeenth century Molière or Racine had been asked why he wrote, no doubt he would have been able to find but one answer; that he wrote "for the entertainment of decent people" (*pour distraire les honnêtes gens*). It is only with the advent of Romanticism that the literary act came to be conceived as a sort of raid on the absolute and its result as a revelation.

Rivière's form of expression is not, to my mind, altogether happy. One might suppose that all that had happened was that a wilful perversity had taken possession of literary men, a new literary disease called Romanticism. That is one of the dangers of expressing one's meaning in terms of "Romanticism": it is a

---

[1] The fact that Johnson was working largely to order only indicates that this historical consciousness was already developed.

term which is constantly changing in different con-
texts, and which is now limited to what appear to be
purely literary and purely local problems, now ex-
panding to cover almost the whole of the life of a time
and of nearly the whole world. It has perhaps not
been observed that in its more comprehensive significance "Romanticism" comes to include nearly everything that distinguishes the last two hundred and
fifty years or so from their predecessors, and includes
so much that it ceases to bring with it any praise or
blame. The change to which Rivière alludes is not
a contrast between Molière and Racine on the one
hand and more modern French writers on the other;
it neither reflects credit upon the former nor implies
inferiority in the latter. In the interest of clarity and
simplicity I wish myself to avoid employing the terms
Romanticism and Classicism, terms which inflame
political passions, and tend to prejudice our conclusions. I am only concerned with my contention that
the notion of what poetry is for, of what is its function
to do, does change, and therefore I quoted Rivière; I
am concerned further with criticism as evidence of the
conception of the use of poetry in the critic's time,
and assert that in order to compare the work of
different critics we must investigate their assumptions
as to what poetry does and ought to do. Examination
of the criticism of our time leads me to believe that we
are still in the Arnold period.

I speak of Mr. Richards's views with some diffi-
dence. Some of the problems he discusses are themselves very difficult, and only those are qualified to

criticise who have applied themselves to the same specialised studies and have acquired proficiency in this kind of thinking. But here I limit myself to passages in which he does not seem to be speaking as a specialist, and in which I have no advantage of special knowledge either. There are two reasons why the writer of poetry must not be thought to have any great advantage. One is that a discussion of poetry such as this takes us far outside the limits within which a poet may speak with authority; the other is that the poet does many things upon instinct, for which he can give no better account than anybody else. A poet can try, of course, to give an honest report of the way in which he himself writes: the result may, if he is a good observer, be illuminating. And in one sense, but a very limited one, he knows better what his poems "mean" than can anyone else; he may know the history of their composition, the material which has gone in and come out in an unrecognisable form, and he knows what he was trying to do and what he was meaning to mean. But what a poem means is as much what it means to others as what it means to the author; and indeed, in the course of time a poet may become merely a reader in respect to his own works, forgetting his original meaning — or without forgetting, merely changing. So that, when Mr. Richards asserts that *The Waste Land* effects "a complete severance between poetry and *all* beliefs" I am no better qualified to say No! than is any other reader. I will admit that I think that either Mr. Richards is wrong, or I do not understand his meaning. The statement might mean that it was the first poetry to do what all poetry in the past would have been the better for doing: I can hardly think that he intended to pay me such an unmerited compliment. It might also mean that the present situation is radically different from any in which poetry has been produced in the past: namely, that now there is nothing in which to believe, that Belief itself is dead; and that therefore my poem is the first to respond properly to the modern situation and not call upon Make-Believe. And it is in this connexion, apparently, that Mr. Richards observes that "poetry is capable of saving us."

A discussion of Mr. Richards's theories of knowledge, value and meaning would be by no means irrelevant to this assertion, but it would take us far afield, and I am not the person to undertake it. We cannot of course refute the statement "poetry is capable of saving us" without knowing which one of the multiple definitions of salvation Mr. Richards has in mind.[1] (A good many people behave as if they thought so too: otherwise their interest in poetry is difficult to explain.) I am sure, from the differences of environment, of period, and of mental furniture, that salvation by poetry is not quite the same thing for Mr. Richards as it was for Arnold; but so far as I am concerned these are merely two variants of one theological error.[2] In *Practical Criticism* [3] Mr. Richards

---

[1] See his *Mencius on the Mind*. There is of course a locution in which we say of someone "he is not one of *us*"; it is possible that the "us" of Mr. Richards's statement represents an equally limited and select number.   [2] And different shades of Blue.

[3] Second Impression, p. 290.

provides a recipe which I think throws some light upon his theological ideas. He says:

Something like a technique or ritual for heightening sincerity might well be worked out. When our response to a poem after our best efforts remains uncertain, when we are unsure whether the feelings it excites come from a deep source in our experience, whether our liking or disliking is genuine, is *ours*, or an accident of fashion, a response to surface details or to essentials, we may perhaps help ourselves by considering it in a frame of feelings whose sincerity is beyond our questioning. Sit by the fire (with eyes shut and fingers pressed firmly upon the eyeballs) and consider with as full "realisation" as possible —

five points which follow, and which I shall comment upon one by one. We may observe, in passing, the intense religious seriousness of Mr. Richards's attitude towards poetry.[1] What he proposes — for he hints in the passage above that his sketch might be elaborated — is nothing less than a regimen of Spiritual Exercises. Now for the points.

I. *Man's loneliness (the isolation of the human situation).*

Loneliness is known as a frequent attitude in romantic poetry, and in the form of "lonesomeness" (as I need not remind American readers) is a frequent

---

[1] This passage is introduced by a long and important discussion of Confucius' conception of "sincerity," which should be read attentively. In passing, it is worthy of remark that Mr. Richards shares his interest in Chinese philosophy with Mr. Ezra Pound and with the late Irving Babbitt. An investigation of an interest common to three apparently quite different thinkers would, I believe, repay the labour. It seems to indicate, at least, a deracination from the Christian tradition. The thought of these three men seems to me to have an interesting similarity.

attitude in contemporary lyrics known as "the blues." But in what sense is Man in general isolated, and from what? What *is* the "human situation"? I can understand the isolation of the human situation as Plato's Diotima expounds it, or in the Christian sense of the separation of Man from God; but not an isolation which is not a separation from anything in particular.

II. *The facts of birth and of death, in their inexplicable oddity.*

I cannot see why the facts of birth and of death should appear odd in themselves, unless we have a conception of some other way of coming into the world and of leaving it, which strikes us as more natural.

III. *The inconceivable immensity of the Universe.*

It was not, we remember, the "immense spaces" themselves but their *eternal silence* that terrified Pascal. With a definite religious background this is intelligible. But the effect of popular astronomy books (like Sir James Jeans's) upon me is only of the insignificance of vast space.

IV. *Man's place in the perspective of time.*

I confess that I do not find this especially edifying either, or stimulating to the imagination, unless I bring to its contemplation some belief that there is a sense and a meaning in the place of human history in the history of the world. I fear that in many people this subject of meditation can only stimulate the idle wonder and greed for facts which are satisfied by Mr. Wells's compendia.

V. *The enormity (sc. enormousness) of man's igno-*
    rance.

Here again, I must ask, ignorance of what? I am acutely aware, for instance, of my own ignorance of specific subjects on which I want to know more; but Mr. Richards does not, surely, mean the ignorance of any individual man, but of *Man*. But "ignorance" must be relative to the sense in which we take the term "knowledge"; and in *Mencius on the Mind* Mr. Richards has given us a useful analysis of the numerous meanings of "knowledge." Mr. Richards, who has engaged in what I believe will be most fruitful investigations of controversy as systematised misunderstanding, may justly be able to accuse me of perverting his meanings. But his modern substitute for the *Exercises* of St. Ignatius is an appeal to our feelings, and I am only trying to set down how they affect mine. To me Mr. Richards's five points only express a modern emotional attitude which I cannot share, and which finds its most sentimental expression in *A Free Man's Worship*. And as the contemplation of Man's place in the Universe has led Lord Russell to write such bad prose, we may wonder whether it will lead the ordinary aspirant to understanding of good poetry. It is just as likely, I suspect, to confirm him in his taste for the second-rate.

I am willing to admit that such an approach to poetry may help some people: my point is that Mr. Richards speaks as though it were good for everybody. I am perfectly ready to concede the existence of people who feel, think and believe as Mr. Richards does in these matters, if he will only concede that there are some people who do not. He told us in *Science and Poetry*:

For centuries ... countless pseudo-statements — about God, about the universe, about human nature, the relations of mind to mind, about the soul, its rank and destiny ... have been believed; now they are gone, irrecoverably; and the knowledge which has killed them is not of a kind upon which an equally fine organisation of the mind can be based.

I submit that this is itself a pseudo-statement, if there is such a thing. But these things are indeed gone, so far as Mr. Richards is concerned, if they are no longer believed by people whose minds Mr. Richards respects: we have no ground for controversy there. I only assert again that what he is trying to do is essentially the same as what Arnold wanted to do: to preserve emotions without the beliefs with which their history has been involved. It would seem that Mr. Richards, on his own showing, is engaged in a rearguard religious action.[1]

Mr. Maritain, with an equally strong conviction that poetry will *not* save us, is equally despondent about the world of to-day. "Could any weakness," he asks, "be greater than the weakness of our contemporaries?" It is no more, as I have said before, the particular business of the poet as poet to concern himself

[1] Somewhat in the spirit of "religion without revelation," of which a greater exponent than Mr. Julian Huxley was Emmanuel Kant. On Kant's attempt (which deeply influenced later German theology) see an illuminating passage in A. E. Taylor's *The Faith of a Moralist*, volume II, chapter ii.

with Maritain's attempt to determine the position of poetry in a Christian world than it is to concern himself with Richards's attempt to determine the position of poetry in a pagan world: but these various ambient ideas get in through the pores, and produce an unsettled state of mind. Trotsky, whose *Literature and Revolution* is the most sensible statement of a Communist attitude that I have seen,[1] is pretty clear on the relation of the poet to his environment. He observes:

Artistic creation is always a complicated turning inside out of old forms, under the influence of new stimuli which originate outside of art. In this large sense of the word, art is a handmaiden. It is not a disembodied element feeding on itself, but a function of social man indissolubly tied to his life and environment.

There is a striking contrast between this conception of art as a handmaiden, and that which we have just observed of art as a saviour. But perhaps the two notions are not so opposed as they appear. Trotsky seems, in any case, to draw the commonsense distinction between art and propaganda, and to be dimly aware that the material of the artist is not his beliefs as *held*, but his beliefs as *felt* (so far as his beliefs are part of his material at all); and he is sensible enough

---

[1] There were also some interesting articles in *The New Republic* by Mr. Edmund Wilson, in controversy (if I remember correctly) with Mr. Michael Gold. I regret that I cannot give the exact reference. The major part of Trotsky's book is not very interesting for those who are unacquainted with the modern Russian authors: one suspects that most of Trotsky's swans are geese.

to see that a period of revolution is not favourable to art, since it puts pressure upon the poet, both direct and indirect, to make him overconscious of his beliefs as *held*. He would not limit communist poetry to the writing of panegyrics upon the Russian State, any more than I should limit Christian poetry to the composition of hymns; the poetry of Villon is just as "Christian" in this way as that of Prudentius or Adam of St. Victor — though I think it would be a long time before Soviet society could afford to approve a Villon, if one arose.[1] It is probable, however, that Russian literature will become increasingly unintelligible, increasingly meaningless, to the peoples of Western Europe unless they develop in the same direction as Russia. Even as things are, in the present chaos of opinion and belief, we may expect to find quite different literatures existing in the same language and the same country. "The unconcealed and palpable influence of the devil on an important part of contemporary literature," says Mr. Maritain, "is one of the significant phenomena of the history of our time." I can hardly expect most of my readers to take this remark seriously;[2] those who do will have very different criteria of criticism from those who do not. Another observation of Mr. Maritain's may be less unacceptable:

[1] The Roman and Communist idea of an index of prohibited books seems to me perfectly sound in principle. It is a question (*a*) of the goodness and universality of the cause, (*b*) of the intelligence that goes to the application.

[2] With the influence of the devil on contemporary literature I shall be concerned in more detail in another book.

By showing us where moral truth and the genuine super-natural are situate, religion saves poetry from the ab-surdity of believing itself destined to transform ethics and life: saves it from overweening arrogance.

This seems to me to be putting the finger on the great weakness of much poetry and criticism of the nine-teenth and twentieth centuries. But between the motive which Rivière attributed to Molière and Racine [1] and the motive of Matthew Arnold bear-ing on shoulders immense what he thought to be the orb of the poet's fate, there is a serious *via media*.

As the doctrine of the moral and educational value of poetry has been elaborated in different forms by Arnold and Mr. Richards, so the Abbé Brémond pre-sented a modern equivalent for the theory of divine inspiration. The task of *Prayer and Poetry* is to estab-lish the likeness, and the difference of kind and de-gree, between poetry and mysticism. In his attempt to demonstrate this relation he safeguards himself by just qualifications, and makes many penetrating re-marks about the nature of poetry. I will confine my-self to two pieces of caution. My first qualm is over the assertion that " the more of a poet any particular poet is, the more he is tormented by the need of com-municating his experience." This is a downright sort of statement which is very easy to accept without examination; but the matter is not so simple as all

[1] Which does not seem to me to cover the case. Let us say that it was the primary motive (even in *Athalie*). An exact statement would need much space; for we cannot concern ourselves only with what went on in-side the poet's head, but with the general state of society.

that. I should say that the poet is tormented primarily by the need to write a poem — and so, I regret to find, are a legion of people who are not poets: so that the line between "need" to write and 'desire" to write is by no means easy to draw. And what is the experience that the poet is so bursting to communicate? By the time it has settled down into a poem it may be so different from the original experience as to be hardly recognisable. The "experience" in question may be the result of a fusion of feelings so numerous, and ultimately so obscure in their origins, that even if there be communication of them, the poet may hardly be aware of what he is communicating; and what is there to be communicated was not in existence before the poem was completed. "Communication" will not explain poetry. I will not say that there is not always some varying degree of communication in poetry, or that poetry could exist without any communication taking place. There is room for very great individual variation in the motives of equally good individual poets; and we have the assurance of Coleridge, with the approval of Mr. Housman, that "poetry gives most pleasure when only generally and not perfectly understood." And I think that my first objection to Brémond's theory is related to the second, in which also the question of motive and intention enters. Any theory which relates poetry very closely to a religious or a social scheme of things aims, probably, to *explain* poetry by discovering its natural laws; but it is in danger of *binding* poetry by legislation — and poetry can recognise no such laws. When the critic falls into this error he has probably done what we all do: when we generalise about poetry, as I have said before, we are generalising from the poetry which we best know and best like; not from all poetry, or even all of the poetry which we have read. What is "all poetry"? Everything written in verse which a sufficient number of the best minds have considered to be poetry. By a sufficient number, I mean enough persons of different types, at different times and places, over a space of time, and including foreigners as well as those to whom the language is native, to cancel every personal bias and eccentricity of taste (for we must all be slightly eccentric in taste to have any taste at all). Now when an account like the Abbé Brémond's is tested by being made itself a test, it tends to reveal some narrowness and exclusiveness; at any rate, a good deal of poetry that I like would be excluded, or given some other name than poetry; just as other writers who like to include much prose as being essentially "poetry" create confusion by including too much. That there is a relation (not necessarily noetic, perhaps merely psychological) between mysticism and some kinds of poetry, or some of the kinds of state in which poetry is produced, I make no doubt. But I prefer not to define, or to test, poetry by means of speculations about its origins; you cannot find a sure test for poetry, a test by which you may distinguish between poetry and mere good verse, by reference to its putative antecedents in the mind of the poet. Brémond seems to me to introduce extra-poetic laws for poetry:

such laws as have been frequently made, and constantly violated.

There is another danger in the association of poetry with mysticism besides that which I have just mentioned, and that of leading the reader to look in poetry for religious satisfactions. These were dangers for the critic and the reader; there is also a danger for the poet. No one can read Mr. Yeats's *Autobiographies* and his earlier poetry without feeling that the author was trying to get as a poet something like the exaltation to be obtained, I believe, from hashish or nitrous oxide. He was very much fascinated by self-induced trance states, calculated symbolism, mediums, theosophy, crystal-gazing, folklore and hobgoblins. Golden apples, archers, black pigs and such paraphernalia abounded. Often the verse has an hypnotic charm: but you cannot take heaven by magic, especially if you are, like Mr. Yeats, a very sane person. Then, by a great triumph of development, Mr. Yeats began to write and is still writing some of the most beautiful poetry in the language, some of the clearest, simplest, most direct.[1]

The number of people capable of appreciating "all poetry" is probably very small, if not merely a theoretical limit; but the number of people who can get *some* pleasure and benefit from some poetry is, I believe, very large. A perfectly satisfactory theory which applied to all poetry would do so only at the

[1] The best analysis of the weakness of Mr. Yeats's poetry that I know is in Mr. Richards's *Science and Poetry*. But I do not think that Mr. Richards quite appreciated Mr. Yeats's later work.

cost of being voided of all content; the more usual reason for the unsatisfactoriness of our theories and general statements about poetry is that while professing to apply to all poetry, they are really theories about, or generalisations from, a limited range of poetry. Even when two persons of taste like the same poetry, this poetry will be arranged in their minds in slightly different patterns; our individual taste in poetry bears the indelible traces of our individual lives with all their experience pleasurable and painful. We are apt either to shape a theory to cover the poetry that we find most moving, or — what is less excusable — to choose the poetry which illustrates the theory we want to hold. You do not find Matthew Arnold quoting Rochester or Sedley. And it is not merely a matter of individual caprice. Each age demands different things from poetry, though its demands are modified, from time to time, by what some new poet has given. So our criticism, from age to age, will reflect the things that the age demands; and the criticism of no one man and of no one age can be expected to embrace the whole nature of poetry or exhaust all of its uses. Our contemporary critics, like their predecessors, are making particular responses to particular situations. No two readers, perhaps, will go to poetry with quite the same demands. Amongst all these demands from poetry and responses to it there is always some permanent element in common, just as there are standards of good and bad writing independent of what any one of us happens to like and dislike; but every effort to formulate the common element is limited by the limitations of particular men in particular places and at particular times; and these limitations become manifest in the perspective of history.

CONCLUSION

I HOPE that I have not given the impression, in this cursory review of theories past and present, that I estimate the value of such theories according to their degree of approximation to some doctrine which I hold myself, and pay them off accordingly. I am too well aware of limitations of interest for which I do not apologise, and of incapacity for abstruse reasoning as well as less pardonable shortcomings. I have no general theory of my own; but on the other hand I would not appear to dismiss the views of others with the indifference which the practitioner may be supposed to feel towards those who theorise about his craft. It is reasonable, I feel, to be on guard against views which claim too much for poetry, as well as to protest against those which claim too little; to recognise a number of uses for poetry, without admitting that poetry must always and everywhere be subservient to any one of them. And while theories of poetry may be tested by their power of refining our sensibility by increasing our understanding, we must not ask that they serve even that purpose of adding to our enjoyment of poetry: any more than we ask of ethical theory that it shall have a direct application to and influence upon human behaviour. Critical speculation, like philosophical speculation and scientific research, must be free to follow its own course; and cannot be called

upon to show immediate results; and I believe that
the pondering (in judicious moderation) of the questions which it raises will tend to enhance our enjoyment.

That there is an analogy between mystical experience and some of the ways in which poetry is written
I do not deny; and I think that the Abbé Brémond
has observed very well the differences as well as the
likenesses; though, as I have said, whether the analogy is of significance for the student of religion, or
only to the psychologist, I do not know. I know, for
instance, that some forms of ill-health, debility or
anaemia, may (if other circumstances are favourable)
produce an efflux of poetry in a way approaching the
condition of automatic writing — though, in contrast
to the claims sometimes made for the latter, the material has obviously been incubating within the poet,
and cannot be suspected of being a present from a
friendly or impertinent demon. What one writes in
this way may succeed in standing the examination of
a more normal state of mind; it gives me the impression, as I have just said, of having undergone a long
incubation, though we do not know until the shell
breaks what kind of egg we have been sitting on.
To me it seems that at these moments, which are char-
acterised by the sudden lifting of the burden of anxi-
ety and fear which presses upon our daily life so
steadily that we are unaware of it, what happens
is something *negative*: that is to say, not "inspiration"
as we commonly think of it, but the breaking down of
strong habitual barriers — which tend to re-form

very quickly.[1] Some obstruction is momentarily whisked away. The accompanying feeling is less like what we know as positive pleasure, than like a sudden relief from an intolerable burden. I agree with Bré-mond, and perhaps go even further, in finding that this disturbance of our quotidian character which re-sults in an incantation, an outburst of words which we hardly recognise as our own (because of the effortless-ness), is a very different thing from mystical illumina-tion. The latter is a vision which may be accompa-nied by the realisation that you will never be able to communicate it to anyone else, or even by the realisa-tion that when it is past you will not be able to recall it to yourself; the former is not a vision but a motion terminating in an arrangement of words on paper.

But I should add one reservation. I should hesitate to say that the experience at which I have hinted is responsible for the creation of all the most profound poetry written, or even always of the best of a single poet's work. For all I know, it may have much more significance for the psychologist's understanding of a particular poet, or of one poet in a certain phase, than

---

[1] I should like to quote a confirmation of my own experience from Mr. A. E. Housman's *Name and Nature of Poetry*: "In short I think that the production of poetry, in its first stage, is less an active than a passive and involuntary process; and if I were obliged, not to define poetry, but to name the class of things to which it belongs, I should call it a secretion; whether a natural secretion, like turpentine in the fir, or a morbid secre-tion, like the pearl in the oyster. I think that my own case, though I may not deal with the matter so cleverly as the oyster does, is the latter; be-cause I have seldom written poetry unless I was rather out of health, and the experience, though pleasurable, was generally agitating and exhaust-ing." I take added satisfaction in the fact that I only read Mr. Hous-man's essay some time after my own lines were written.

it has for anyone's understanding of poetry. Some finer minds, indeed, may operate very differently; I cannot think of Shakespeare or Dante as having been dependent upon such capricious releases. Perhaps this throws no light on poetry at all. I am not even sure that the poetry which I have written in this way is the best that I have written; and so far as I know, no critic has ever identified the passages I have in mind. The way in which poetry is written is not, so far as our knowledge of these obscure matters as yet extends, any clue to its value. But, as Norton wrote in a letter to Dr. L. P. Jacks in 1907, "I have no belief that such views as mine are likely within any reasonable time to be held by a considerable body of men"; for people are always ready to grasp at any guide which will help them to recognise the best poetry without having to depend upon their own sensibility and taste. The faith in mystical inspiration is responsible for the exaggerated repute of *Kubla Khan*. The imagery of that fragment, certainly, whatever its origins in Coleridge's reading, sank to the depths of Coleridge's feeling, was saturated, transformed there — "those are pearls that were his eyes" — and brought up into daylight again. But it is not *used*: the poem has not been written. A single verse is not poetry unless it is a one-verse poem; and even the finest line draws its life from its context. Organisation is necessary as well as "inspiration." The re-creation of word and image which happens fitfully in the poetry of such a poet as Coleridge happens almost incessantly with Shakespeare. Again and again, in his use of a word, he will give a new meaning or extract a latent one; again and again the right imagery, saturated while it lay in the depths of Shakespeare's memory, will rise like Anadyomene from the sea. In Shakespeare's poetry this reborn image or word will have its rational use and justification; in much good poetry the organisation will not reach to so rational a level. I will take an example which I have used elsewhere: I am glad of the opportunity to use it again, as on the previous occasion I had an inaccurate text. It is from Chapman's *Bussy D'Ambois*:

> Fly where the evening from the Iberian vales
> Takes on her swarthy shoulders Hecate
> Crowned with a grove of oaks: fly where men feel
> The burning axletree, and those that suffer
> Beneath the chariot of the snowy Bear . . .

Chapman borrowed this, as Dr. Boas points out, from Seneca's *Hercules Œteus*:

> dic sub Aurora positis Sabaeis
> dic sub occasu positis Hiberis
> quique sub plaustro patiuntur ursae
> quique ferventi quatiuntur axe

and probably also from the same author's *Hercules Furens*:

> sub ortu solis, an sub cardine
> glacialis ursae?

There is first the probability that this imagery had some personal saturation value, so to speak, for Seneca; another for Chapman, and another for myself, who have borrowed it twice from Chapman. I suggest that what gives it such intensity as it has in each case is its saturation — I will not say with "associations," for I do not want to revert to Hartley — but with feelings too obscure for the authors even to know quite what they were. And of course only a part of an author's imagery comes from his reading. It comes from the whole of his sensitive life since early childhood. Why, for all of us, out of all that we have heard, seen, felt, in a lifetime, do certain images recur, charged with emotion, rather than others? The song of one bird, the leap of one fish, at a particular place and time, the scent of one flower, an old woman on a German mountain path, six ruffians seen through an open window playing cards at night at a small French railway junction where there was a water-mill: such memories may have symbolic value, but of what we cannot tell, for they come to represent the depths of feeling into which we cannot peer. We might just as well ask why, when we try to recall visually some period in the past, we find in our memory just the few meagre arbitrarily chosen set of snapshots that we do find there, the faded poor souvenirs of passionate moments.[1]

Thus far is as far as my experience will take me in this direction. My purpose has not been to examine thoroughly any one type of theory of poetry, still less

[1] In Chapter XXII of *Principles of Literary Criticism* Mr. Richards discusses these matters in his own way. As evidence that there are other approaches as well, see a very interesting article, *Le symbolisme et l'âme primitive*, by E. Cailliet and J. A. Bédé, in the *Revue de litterature comparée* for April–June 1932. The authors, who have done field work in Madagascar, apply the theories of Lévy-Bruhl: the pre-logical mentality persists in civilised man, but becomes available only to or through the poet.

to confute it; but rather to indicate the kinds of defect and excess that we must expect to find in each, and to suggest that the current tendency is to expect too much, rather than too little, of poetry. No one of us, when he thinks about poetry, is without his own bias; and Abbé Brémond's preoccupation with mysticism and Mr. Richards's lack of interest in theology are equally significant. One voice was raised, in our time, to express a view of a different kind; that of a man who wrote several remarkable poems himself, and who also had an aptitude for theology. It is that of T. E. Hulme:

There is a general tendency to think that verse means little else than the expression of unsatisfied emotion. People say: "But how can you have verse without sentiment?" You see what it is; the prospect alarms them. A classical revival to them would mean the prospect of an arid desert and the death of poetry as they understand it, and could only come to fill the gulf caused by that death. Exactly why this dry classical spirit should have a positive and legitimate necessity to express itself in poetry is utterly inconceivable to them. . . . The great aim is accurate, precise and definite description. The first thing is to realise how extraordinarily difficult this is. . . . Language has its own special nature, its own conventions and communal ideas. It is only by a concentrated effort of the mind that you can hold it fixed to your own purpose.

This is, we must remark at once, not a general theory of poetry, but an assertion of the claims of a particular kind of poetry for the writer's own time. It may serve to remind us how various are the kinds of poetry, and how variously poetry may appeal to different minds and generations equally qualified to appreciate it.

The extreme of theorising about the nature of poetry, the essence of poetry if there is any, belongs to the study of aesthetics and is no concern of the poet or of a critic with my limited qualifications. Whether the self-consciousness involved in aesthetics and in psychology does not risk violating the frontier of consciousness is a question which I need not raise here; it is perhaps only my private eccentricity to believe that such researches are perilous if not guided by sound theology. The poet is much more vitally concerned with the social "uses" of poetry, and with his own place in society; and this problem is now perhaps more importunately pressed upon his conscious attention than at any previous time. The uses of poetry certainly vary as society alters, as the public to be addressed changes. In this context something should be said about the vexed question of obscurity and unintelligibility. The difficulty of poetry (and modern poetry is supposed to be difficult) may be due to one of several reasons. First, there may be personal causes which make it impossible for a poet to express himself in any but an obscure way; while this may be regrettable, we should be glad, I think, that the man has been able to express himself at all. Or difficulty may be due just to novelty: we know the ridicule accorded in turn to Wordsworth, Shelley and Keats, Tennyson and Browning — but must remark that Browning was the first to be *called* difficult; hostile critics of the earlier poets found them difficult, but called them silly. Or difficulty may be caused by the reader's having been told, or having suggested to himself, that the poem is going to prove difficult. The ordinary reader, when warned against the obscurity of a poem, is apt to be thrown into a state of consternation very unfavourable to poetic receptivity. Instead of beginning, as he should, in a state of sensitivity, he obfuscates his senses by the desire to be clever and to look very hard for something, he doesn't know what — or else by the desire not to be taken in. There is such a thing as stage fright, but what such readers have is pit or gallery fright. The more seasoned reader, he who has reached, in these matters, a state of greater *purity*, does not bother about understanding; not, at least, at first. I know that some of the poetry to which I am most devoted is poetry which I did not understand at first reading; some is poetry which I am not sure I understand yet: for instance, Shakespeare's. And finally, there is the difficulty caused by the author's having left out something which the reader is used to finding; so that the reader, bewildered, gropes about for what is absent, and puzzles his head for a kind of "meaning" which is not there, and is not meant to be there.

The chief use of the "meaning" of a poem, in the ordinary sense, may be (for here again I am speaking of some kinds of poetry and not all) to satisfy one habit of the reader, to keep his mind diverted and quiet, while the poem does its work upon him: much as the imaginary burglar is always provided with a bit of nice meat for the house-dog. This is a normal situation of which I approve. But the minds of all poets do not work that way; some of them, assuming that there are other minds like their own, become impatient of this "meaning" which seems superfluous, and perceive possibilities of intensity through its elimination. I am not asserting that this situation is ideal; only that we must write our poetry as we can, and take it as we find it. It may be that for some periods of society a more relaxed form of writing is right, and for others a more concentrated. I believe that there must be many people who feel, as I do, that the effect of some of the greater nineteenth-century poets is diminished by their bulk. Who now, for the pure pleasure of it, reads Wordsworth, Shelley and Keats even, certainly Browning and Swinburne and most of the French poets of the century — entire? I by no means believe that the "long poem" is a thing of the past; but at least there must be more in it for the length than our grandparents seemed to demand; and for us, anything that can be said as well in prose can be said better in prose. And a great deal, in the way of meaning, belongs to prose rather than to poetry. The doctrine of "art for art's sake," a mistaken one, and more advertised than practised, contained this true impulse behind it, that it is a recognition of the error of the poet's trying to do other people's work. But poetry has as much to learn from prose as from other poetry; and I think that an interaction between prose and verse, like the interaction between language and language, is a condition of vitality in literature.

To return to the question of obscurity: when all exceptions have been made, and after admitting the possible existence of minor "difficult" poets whose public must always be small, I believe that the poet naturally prefers to write for as large and miscellaneous an audience as possible, and that it is the half-educated and ill-educated, rather than the uneducated, who stand in his way: I myself should like an audience which could neither read nor write.[1] The most useful poetry, socially, would be one which could cut across all the present stratifications of public taste—stratifications which are perhaps a sign of social disintegration. The ideal medium for poetry, to my mind, and the most direct means of social "usefulness" for poetry, is the theatre. In a play of Shakespeare you get several levels of significance. For the simplest auditors there is the plot, for the more thoughtful the character and conflict of character, for the more literary the words and phrasing, for the more musically sensitive the rhythm, and for auditors of greater sensitiveness and understanding a meaning which reveals itself gradually. And I do not believe that the classification of audience is so clear-cut as this; but rather that the sensitiveness of every auditor is acted upon by all these elements at once, though in different degrees of consciousness. At none of these levels is the auditor bothered by the presence of that which he does not understand, or by the presence of that in which he is not interested. I may make my meaning a little clearer by a simple instance. I once designed, and

[1] On the subject of education, there are some helpful remarks in Lawrence's *Fantasia of the Unconscious*.

drafted a couple of scenes, of a verse play. My intention was to have one character whose sensibility and intelligence should be on the plane of the most sensitive and intelligent members of the audience; his speeches should be addressed to them as much as to the other personages in the play — or rather, should be addressed to the latter who were to be material, literal-minded and visionless, with the consciousness of being overheard by the former. There was to be an understanding between this protagonist and a small number of the audience, while the rest of the audience would share the responses of the other characters in the play. Perhaps this is all too deliberate, but one must experiment as one can.

Every poet would like, I fancy, to be able to think that he had some direct social utility. By this, as I hope I have already made clear, I do not mean that he should meddle with the tasks of the theologian, the preacher, the economist, the sociologist or anybody else; that he should do anything but write poetry, poetry not defined in terms of something else. He would like to be something of a popular entertainer, and be able to think his own thoughts behind a tragic or a comic mask. He would like to convey the pleasures of poetry, not only to a larger audience, but to larger groups of people collectively; and the theatre is the best place in which to do it. There might, one fancies, be some fulfilment in exciting this communal pleasure, to give an immediate compensation for the pains of turning blood into ink. As things are, and as fundamentally they must always be, poetry is not a career, but a mug's game. No honest poet can ever feel quite sure of the permanent value of what he has written: he may have wasted his time and messed up his life for nothing. All the better, then, if he could have at least the satisfaction of having a part to play in society as worthy as that of the music-hall comedian. Furthermore, the theatre, by the technical exactions which it makes and limitations which it imposes upon the author, by the obligation to keep for a definite length of time the sustained interest of a large and unprepared and not wholly perceptive group of people, by its problems which have constantly to be solved, has enough to keep the poet's *conscious* mind fully occupied, as the painter's by the manipulation of his tools. If, beyond keeping the interest of a crowd of people for that length of time, the author can make a play which is real poetry, so much the better.

I have not attempted any definition of poetry, because I can think of none which does not assume that the reader already knows what it is, or which does not falsify by leaving out much more than it can include. Poetry begins, I dare say, with a savage beating a drum in a jungle, and it retains that essential of percussion and rhythm; hyperbolically one might say that the poet is *older* than other human beings — but I do not want to be tempted to ending on this sort of flourish. I have insisted rather on the variety of poetry, variety so great that all the kinds seem to have nothing in common except the rhythm of verse instead of the rhythm of prose: and that does not tell you much about all poetry. Poetry is of course not to be defined by its uses. If it commemorates a public occasion, or celebrates a festival, or decorates a religious rite, or amuses a crowd, so much the better. It may effect revolutions in sensibility such as are periodically needed; may help to break up the conventional modes of perception and valuation which are perpetually forming, and make people see the world afresh, or some new part of it. It may make us from time to time a little more aware of the deeper, unnamed feelings which form the substratum of our being, to which we rarely penetrate; for our lives are mostly a constant evasion of ourselves, and an evasion of the visible and sensible world. But to say all this is only to say what you know already, if you have felt poetry and thought about your feelings. And I fear that I have already, throughout these lectures, trespassed beyond the bounds which a little self-knowledge tells me are my proper frontier. If, as James Thomson observed, "lips only sing when they cannot kiss," it may also be that poets only talk when they cannot sing. I am content to leave my theorising about poetry at this point. The sad ghost of Coleridge beckons to me from the shadows.